COME
CELEBRATE
WITH US

A Church
on Peachtree

COME
CELEBRATE
WITH US

TUESDAYS
Worship 9:15 am
Bible Study 9:30 am

WEDNESDAYS
Dinner 5:00 pm
Program 6:30 pm

PRESCHOOL
9:00 am-12:00 Weekdays

CHURCH SCHOOL
Childcare Available
10:05 am

A Church on Peachtree

First Presbyterian Church
of Atlanta
A Sesquicentennial Story

1848-1998

Beth Dawkins Bassett

The Church in the Heart of the City

Reaching Out to the World

1998-2011

Gayle White

Editor, Rob Levin
Editorial Associates, Cheryl Sadler and Renée Peyton
New Photography, Ken Hawkins
Project Directors, Anne Murdoch and Renée Peyton
Book Design, Paulette Livers Lambert
Jacket Design, Stateless Design
Copyediting, Indexing, and Appendix, Bob Land
First Presbyterian Church of Atlanta Liaison, Sal Kibler

Copyright © 1998, 2011 by First Presbyterian Church of Atlanta
PO Box 77005
Atlanta, GA 30357

Second Edition

Printed in the U.S.A.

Book Development by Bookhouse Group, Inc.
818 Marietta Street
Atlanta, GA 30318
404.885.9515
www.bookhouse.net

Book Committee
Cindy Candler
Karna Candler
David Gambrell
Sal Kibler
Leila Taratus
Gayle White
Dr. George B. Wirth

Book Advisory Committee, First Edition
William and Lucy Emerson*
Dr. Harry Fifield*
Franklin Garrett*
Louise Grant
Arthur Howell*
Barbara Hull
Melissa Hurt*
McChesney Jeffries*
A.B. Padgett*
William Pressly*
Frank Walsh III

* Deceased

"God has gotten right down into our experience—with us who live and love and cry and die along Peachtree Street."
—Dr. Harry A. Fifield

Contents

Mrs. Laura Hill Boland

Foreword

by William L. Pressly

This history of the First Presbyterian Church of Atlanta is dedicated to the glory of God and in loving memory and admiration of Laura Hill Boland, a loyal member of the church throughout her life, who made this book possible with her generous bequest to the church. Regular in her attendance, Laura loved beauty and worshipfulness, as was evident in her admiration for our magnificent sanctuary. Her love of beauty also prompted her to support the High Museum, both as generous benefactor and faithful volunteer. In this effort, she followed the lead of her father, Walter C. Hill, a prominent businessman and member of First Church, who was one of the museum's first presidents. The museum expressed its appreciation by establishing the Walter C. Hill Auditorium.

We are deeply grateful to Laura and her children, Laura and Joseph, for making this history possible, for First Church is eminently worthy of recognition.

Founded in 1848, First Church has always based its belief on faith in Jesus Christ, the Son of God, and God's revelation of Himself to humanity. The exquisite stained-glass windows in the sanctuary are sacred symbols of great beauty, developed under the direction of Dr. J. Sprole Lyons, who conceived the windows as portraying God's revelation of Himself to mankind

from the call of Abraham; through the birth, life, death, and Resurrection of Jesus Christ; to Christ's Ascension and Second Coming in glory and majesty. The summation of Christ's present position is presented in the Rose Window over the chancel, depicting Christ sitting on the rainbow in heaven with golden rays of influence emanating from Him throughout the universe and with angels all around Him playing trumpets, lyres, cymbals, and tambourines while perhaps singing "Gloria in Excelsis Deo."

Ours is a great church, growing rapidly, welcoming all believers and devoting much attention to community service. Down through the generations, worshippers have remained true to the faith and in dignity and joy have praised God in song, prayer, Scripture reading, and sermon every Sunday for these 150 years.

The congregation and staff are dedicated to keeping our faith and worship flourishing for centuries to come. In making the publication of this history a reality, Laura Boland has made it possible for all who worship here in the future to know why our church is such a holy place to those of us who have gone before, including the great "cloud of witnesses" and the communion of saints.

Left: The Abrahamic Covenant
Facing page: Christ's Life and Ministry

Chapter 1

A Church on Peachtree

*"So then, you are no longer
strangers and sojourners,
but you are fellow citizens with
the saints and members of the
household of God, . . ."*
Ephesians 2:19

n this Sabbath morning, the sanctuary of the First Presbyterian Church of Atlanta is filled with a hum of sound, words indistinguishable, as worshippers greet each other just outside the doors. Once they enter the sacred place, they face the dais where eleven scarlet-cushioned apostles' chairs and the central pulpit stand. Above the dais is an intensely colored stained-glass rose window depicting Christ enthroned in glory. To the left and right, lining the sanctuary walls on either side and dominating the room, are ten tall, rectangular stained-glass windows, also vividly colored, that chronicle humankind's journey with God from the time of Abraham through the birth, ministry, passion, and Resurrection of Christ and the spread of Christianity. On the rear wall of the sanctuary is the climactic eleventh window showing the moment of Christ's Second Coming. In this window, the triumphantly returned Christ is surrounded by light, and one of his feet has yet to touch Earth.

Presently, chimes sound the hour and the organ begins a familiar old hymn tune: "O God, our Help in ages past, Our Hope for years to come, Our Shelter from the stormy blast, And our eternal Home." As the sound of the organ softens, the sweet voices of children begin to sing a Jubilate Deo. The date is May 19, 1996, and this is the beginning of a service rededicating the sanctuary that has stood at the corner of Sixteenth and Peachtree Streets since 1919.

Today's service celebrating the completion of renovation begun in the fall of 1995 included many reminders of the 1919 dedication service. Today, as on April 6, 1919, the Bible is brought down the aisle to the pulpit in the traditional Scottish way, and Jane Carter, chairperson of the renovation project, and William Lyons, grandson of Dr. J. Sprole Lyons under whose ministry the Peachtree building was constructed, help lead the same responsive reading his grandfather led seventy-seven years ago. Today, as then, the people receive the timeless

A Stone From Ephesus

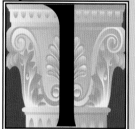

In 1910, William J. Ellis, a newspaper writer from Swarthmore, Pennsylvania, visited the Greek city of Ephesus, said to have been settled before 1000 B.C., site both of the ancient Greek temple of Diana and one of the earliest churches of Christendom, the Double Church of Saint John the Divine. During his visit, Ellis came upon a stone on which a cross was carved in relief. The stone would later become a valued part of First Church.

It was the Apostle Paul who brought Christianity to Ephesus during his missionary journeys, and to the congregation there was addressed the New Testament Letter to the Ephesians. Tradition suggests that John the Elder also spent time in the city during the latter part of his life and wrote the first of the letters in the book of Revelation there.

At the time of Ellis's visit, little remained of the Greek temple. But the white marble walls of the Double Church of Saint John the Divine still stood, albeit untended and virtually in the midst of plowed field.

"I found crude farming going on right up to the walls of the church," Ellis later said. "As I was leaving the church, riding over a plowed field that adjoined it. I noticed lying by a furrow, and just about to be turned under by the next plow, a small block of marble, containing a cross, which had been part of the walls or ornamentation of the church, and had fallen to the ground. As the block of marble was not attached to the walls . . . and as its loose condition would make it fair spoil for one of the lime-burners who have destroyed so many priceless marble, I made signs to my horse-boy that if he would convey the block of marble to Smyrna [Turkey], I would pay him for it."

In Smyrna, one of Ellis's friends arranged for the marble to be shipped to New Jersey, and from there Ellis took it to his home in Swarthmore.

After keeping the marble for several years, Ellis, on a lecture visit to First Church in 1917, gave it to Dr. Lyons to by used in the new sanctuary. Lyons, in turn, commissioned The Tiffany Studios in New York City to use the stone as part of a baptismal font, and they mounted it on a low, matching marble pedestal.

"I am very proud of the skill with which Tiffany mounted the relic," Ellis later wrote First Church. "I had cudgeled my brains in vain to devise a mounting that would not be incongruous. . . . I have always been glad that I gave it to you, and not to a museum."

message that the love of God in Jesus Christ overarches humanity's turbulent history.

Today, First Presbyterian Church stands at the heart of a bustling city, but in 1919, it was located in the midst of a quiet residential area, having been built "pretty far out" at the corner of Peachtree and Sixteenth Streets, according to session minutes, on "a vacant lot." The Peachtree location was the third of the church's history. Its two previous buildings stood on Marietta Street, nearer the original nucleus of the city, the first having been completed in 1852 and the second on the same site in 1879.

But the church's history reaches further back in time. The congregation that built its churches on Marietta Street grew out of a small nondenominational group of Christians who first met in a log cabin in Atlanta when the city had only twenty-five hundred bustling inhabitants, many so new to the settlement they still lived in shanties in the woods. In 1848, the nineteen Presbyterians attending the little Union Church formed the Presbyterian Church of Atlanta, and in 1858 that church was divided into two congregations, one called "The First Presbyterian Church of Atlanta."

Over the years, the life of the church has proceeded against the backdrop of the history of Atlanta, the nation, and the world. In 1863, fifteen years after the original body was organized, the Civil War that had largely been fought outside Georgia came to the state's doorsteps when Union forces captured Chattanooga, spilled into Georgia, and lurched toward Atlanta. During the Battle of Atlanta, fought during the summer of 1864, a dozen or more shells hit what accounts call "the old war church" the Presbyterians had built on Marietta Street. Among those killed during the battle was the physician son of the founding pastor of the church, Dr. John S. Wilson.

In 1917, as the church met in the Sunday School building completed on Peachtree in 1915, the United States entered World War I, and in 1929, the year of the stock market crash that would usher in the Great Depression, the church completed an addition to its Peachtree structure to house more Sunday School rooms. On September 3, 1939, the day England's declaration of war on Germany brought the world to the brink of World War II, WSB radio suspended its broadcasts of First Presbyterian's Sunday morning service for the first time since they had been instituted in 1922.

During World War II, the church prayed for members serving in the armed forces and ministered to wounded servicemen hospitalized in the city. On the evening of D-Day, June 6, 1944, the church held a prayer service, not knowing whether the Allied invasion of Normandy would succeed or how many of their relatives and friends would be wounded or die in France. On August 15, 1945, members met to celebrate the end of the war and the long season of sacrifice, and as part of the centennial celebration in 1948, the church dedicated a choir program to the memory of organist Charles Sheldon's son and the nine other members who had died in the war.

First Church's connection with the nation's history continued in 1954, nine decades after the Battle of Atlanta, when the Supreme Court decision in *Brown v. the Board of Education of Topeka (Kansas)* struck down racial segregation in the public schools. This decision began a series of events that would again play themselves out in part in Atlanta. Responding to that ruling, the Southern Presbyterian Church sent letters to individual congregations asking them to take a Christian stand in matters of race relations. After intense discussion, the session of First Church voted to admit black Christians to worship services as they would any others. In 1957, the pastor, Dr. Harry Fifield, along with eighty other ministers, issued an Atlanta Ministers' Manifesto calling for the preservation of the public schools and obedience to the country's laws.

In 1958, in the midst of the general turmoil that followed the Supreme Court ruling, the Jewish Temple at Peachtree and Spring Streets was bombed. First Church invited that congregation to worship at their facility, and they did so until the Temple was restored. After civil rights leader Dr. Martin Luther King Jr. was killed on April 4, 1968, the church housed many of the people who came to the city for the funeral and helped provide food for many others. In 1973, the church received its first black member since the days of slavery.

In the 1960s and 1970s, First Church responded to members of the alternative hippie culture that began to concentrate around Tenth Street. Members and staff ministered to the young people in various ways, including the assumption of primary sponsorship of Aurora House, located on Tenth Street, which offered counseling, Bible study, and practical necessities such as showers and washing machines. As the hippie culture died out and the number of homeless people increased in the area, the church extended its ministry to include them and also widened its ministry to international students and immigrants finding their way to Atlanta in increasing numbers.

First Church means many things to many people. For some, it is both the church of their youth and the church their families have attended since Atlanta's earliest days. For some, it is a church that has stood solidly and with continuity of purpose through changing times. For some, it is an open door on Peachtree.

And for some it literally is home. Dr. George B. Wirth met a woman for whom the church was home soon after he came as pastor in 1990. "We had a dinner for new members," he recalled. "People were introduced and their addresses were listed on a white sheet of paper. The person introducing new members that night said, 'I would like you to meet' and she gave her name. Then she said, 'I'm going to let her say some things about herself.' The woman got up and repeated her name, and then she said, 'My home is the corner of Sixteenth and Peachtree.'

"I realized that this was, in my short tenure, an example of a woman who had come to our Women's Shelter, stayed longer than most, felt welcome here, and joined this church."

In his rededication sermon on May 19, 1996, Dr. Wirth read from Paul's letter to the Ephesians:

> *So, then, you are no longer strangers and sojourners, but you are fellow citizens with the saints and members of the household of God, built upon the foundation of the apostles and prophets, Christ Jesus Himself being the cornerstone, in whom the whole structure is joined together and grows into a Holy Temple for the Lord; in whom you also are built into it for a dwelling place of God in the Spirit.*

Members of First Church open a time capsule on May 19, 1996. The capsule was installed with the best intentions on April 6, 1919, but upon inspecting its contents it was obvious that none of the artifacts had stood the test of time as well as the church had.

The Great Window Spaces

When Dr. J. Sprole Lyons, the Building Committee, and architect W. T. Downing planned the sanctuary to be built on Peachtree Street, they decided that eleven large openings, five down both sides and one at the rear, would be left for stained-glass windows to be designed and installed as members of the congregation gave money for their execution. This proposal was "fully discussed," Dr. Lyons wrote, "all but deciding just what would be a suitable subject or theme for each of the great window spaces."

The more he thought about it, the more Dr. Lyons believed that the windows "appealed for someone to be their advocate," and the more he became convinced that he must become that advocate. He worked with several possible themes, and decided that the best was "the historical steps or stages in the outworking of the Plan of Salvation . . . from the declaration of God's purpose to [Abraham] to its glorious consummation in the gathering of the redeemed in the heavenly home."

Obtaining sanction of this theme from church officers, he began working with artists at The Tiffany Studios in New York City, and often with Louis C. Tiffany himself, slowly laying out plans for the story each window would tell. It was decided that the window would lead the mind and eye both backward and forward in time. For example, Moses, David, and Isaiah in the Law, The Psalms, The Prophets Window would look directly toward the Christ Child in the Advent Window, and below the Advent Window, the small central symbol would be a tablet of stone, a harp, and a prophet's mantle. It was also decided the Passion Window would portray Christ in the Garden of Gethsemane and not on the cross of Calvary. This choice was made, Dr. Lyons's son wrote, because his father believed that in Gethsemane Jesus actually endured the agony of submitting to the cross; that there the "human was sublimated into the Divine, and Christ the Savior, the Son of God, went on to the cross, calm, collected, willing."

The Tiffany Studios executed six of the windows before the company

10

was dissolved after the death of Louis Tiffany in 1933. The D'Ascenzo Studios in Philadelphia executed the next four windows, and the Willett Studios, also in Philadelphia, made the eleventh, The Second Coming of Jesus Christ. On May 3, 1922, a Willett-Studios-designed twelfth circular window was installed above the organ pipes at the front of the sanctuary.

Of all the windows, Dr. Lyons had the most difficulty with the Advent picture. The problem was that the Tiffany artists "insisted on representing [the Infant Jesus] as a little, mature old man sitting on Mary's knee, and preaching, performing miracles etc.," Dr. Lyons wrote. "I explained to them that the child Jesus must be represented as a normal little Babe, nesting in His Mother's arm. . . . They renewed their . . . efforts to sketch an infant child Jesus; but all failed again. Finally, I suggested to Mr. Tiffany that he send two or three artists to a hospital, and ask a nurse to let them see a recently born babe for a model. There was a chorus of 'Ah! That is great.' And without further delay they sketched several very lovely and appropriate baby pictures!"

The Advent

Following pages: In 1931, First Church entered into a contract with the Ecclesiastical Department of Tiffany Studios in New York to execute The Advent window for the sanctuary at a cost of $10,000, made available through the generosity of Mrs. D.R. Peteet. Other sanctuary windows were given by Frank P. Phillips (The Abrahamic Covenant), the George W. Harrison estate (The Law, The Psalms, The Prophets), Mr. and Mrs. Ernest Woodruff (Christ's Life and Ministry), Mrs. William T. Healey (The Passion), Mrs. John W. Grant and Mrs. Hugh Richardson (The Resurrection), Mrs. Samuel M. Inman (The Ascension), W.R. Hoyt and family (Pentecost), Mrs. James D. Robinson and Mrs. Gordon P. Kiser (Christian Martyrs), the congregation in tribute to Dr. and Mrs. Lyons (Christian Missions), James D. Robinson (Christ's Return), and the family of Frank Carter (The Rose Window).

TIFFANY ⑤ STVDIOS

ECCLESIASTICAL DEPARTMENT

46 WEST TWENTY-THIRD STREET

NEW YORK

ORIGINAL

LOUIS C. TIFFANY
President and Art Director

EDWIN STANTON GEORGE
2nd Vice-President and Manager

DESIGNERS AND MAKERS OF
STAINED GLASS
WINDOWS AND MOSAICS
INDOOR MEMORIALS
OUTDOOR MEMORIALS
CHURCH FURNISHINGS

January 9th, 1931.

For the sum of TEN THOUSAND . . . . Dollars ($ 10,000.00

we agree to execute, furnish and deliver at First Presbyterian Church,

Atlanta, Georgia

on or before .... in compliance with this agreement, and the sketches or

designs, if any, submitted and approved, and the description and specifications here following, the glass work now mentioned, to wit:

Window similar to that depicted on colored sketch approved by you,
setting forth scene of the Nativity and Epiphany, including suitable text and inscription, ventilator and protection glass, all
set complete in the above mentioned church.
Full size drawing to be approved by you or Dr. J. Sprole Lyons
before actual execution of the window is taken in hand.

SPECIFICATIONS

In general	The work shall be executed in a substantial manner and be free from defects in material and workmanship.
	The coloring of the work shall be a true and fair interpretation of the spirit of the sketch or color design.
Glass	The glass used shall be of such quality as will, in the exercise of the discretion of the Art Director of this Company, MR. LOUIS C. TIFFANY, produce the best effect.
Leading	All leading shall be soldered on both sides with the best solder.
Cementing	All leaded work shall be thoroughly cemented with the best waterproof cement.
Barring and Wiring	All glass shall be provided with a sufficient number of amply strong bars of galvanized iron, with proper and sufficient copper wires firmly soldered to the lead work.
Iron Frames	If iron frames are specified, they shall be of wrought iron, with ample strength to resist any wind pressure.

Ventilators	If ventilators are specified, they shall be made of galvanized iron, and of ample strength to resist wind pressure.
Outside Protection Glass	If outside glass is specified, it shall be of a heavy, rough, ribbed-plate glass and shall be properly set and embedded in the rebates supplied by you.
Painting	All heads, hands, figures, architectural ornament, etc., and such other detail as may require painting, shall be burned or fused into the surface of the glass.
Inscription and Text	Any inscription or text to be placed upon the window, or windows, is to be formally approved in writing.
Payments Terms	One-half the contract price shall be paid on the completion of the cutting of the glass, and the balance upon final completion of the work. Should we be delayed in shipping or completing the work, by reason of any fault on your part, all payments shall become due and payable upon the performance by us of our part of the contract, and any deferred payment shall bear interest at the rate of 6 per cent per annum from the date of such completion.
	Until the final payment in full shall have been made we retain a first and valid lien upon all the work furnished by us, and shall have the right at all times prior to such final payment upon failure on owner's part to make all payment as hereinbefore provided, to take possession of and remove same, and to retain possession thereof in liquidation of damages for the non-fulfilment of contract on your part.
Verbal Agreements	It is hereby expressly understood and agreed that any and all verbal agreements, statements or representations made by any person or persons for or on behalf of the parties hereto shall not affect this indenture unless written acknowledgment of same, signed by all parties, is added hereto.
Time of Completion	The entire work will be completed by the time first stated, unless alterations are required, or delays caused by strikes, or other unforeseen causes beyond our control.
Price	The price named shall cover only such work as is necessary to properly execute and complete the work here specified and described, and a charge will be made for such additional work as we are asked to supply.
Special Conditions	This work is to be inspected and approved at the Studios before shipment, and no change shall be made after the same is completed and set in place without the approval of Mr. Louis C. Tiffany, and for which an extra charge will be made.

TIFFANY STVDIOS

Witness:

Emile Schuld *Chas. W. Nussbaum*

ACCEPTANCE

The foregoing indenture is hereby accepted this *Jan. 23rd* .... day

of .... 193..., in all particulars.

Witness:

J. Sprole Lyous *Mrs J. M. High*

Chapter II

By the Providence of God Assembled

"We, therefore, whose names are hereunto subscribed, being by the Providence of God assembled in this place . . . do agree to unite in the organization of a church to be known as 'The Presbyterian Church of Atlanta.'"

—From the original Declaration of Rules

Preceding page: The original home of First Church was completed in 1852. The austere but handsome structure stood on Marietta Street.

The Presbyterians and all other Christians in Atlanta first worshipped in this log cabin, which also housed the Male Academy. It was built in 1847 in a chinquapin thicket that stood in the triangle now formed by Pryor, Houston, and Peachtree Streets. In those days the settlement that would become Atlanta comprised a few cabins, and the price of choice lots was $50.

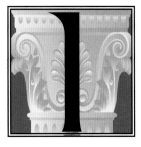n 1847, according to a journal entry written by educator Dr. William N. White, newly arrived in Atlanta from Utica, New York, settlers were flocking to the settlement and most were either busily building or busily planning to build, as Atlantans have been doing ever since. Purposeful chaos reigned. "187 buildings have been put up this summer within eight months," the young schoolteacher wrote on October 21, "and more are in progress. The woods all around are full of shanties, and the merchants live in them until they can find time to build. The streets are still full of stumps and roots; large chestnut and oak logs are scattered about, but the streets are alive and the stores are full of trade and bustle. . . . I have only been here two days and am becoming quite an old settler. The people here bow and shake hands with everybody they meet, as there are so many coming in all the time that they cannot remember with whom they are acquainted. . . ."

Surrounding the commotion was a setting of great beauty. "Much [of it] was a forest," wrote Methodist minister George Gilman Smith in "Recollections of An Atlanta Boy 1847 to 1855," published in the *Atlanta Journal* in 1909. "The young timber had been cut out for wood and the pines for lumber, and the beautiful oaks formed a great park. . . . I never saw more beauty than there was in the springtime in the groves all over Atlanta. All the undergrowth except the azaleas and dogwoods had been cut out. The sward was covered with the fairest woodland flowers, phloxes, lilies, trilliums, violets, pink roots, primroses. . . . Honeysuckles of every hue . . . were in lavish luxuriance. The white dogwood was everywhere; the red woodbine and now and then a yellow jessamine climbed on the trees. Then a stream was found it was clear as crystal."

According to Smith, the limits of the city extended one mile in each direction from "the Union Station, or as it was then called, the car shed." Within the city, White wrote, were twenty-five hundred people and thirty stores, two hotels, three newspapers, and two schools. "Not a church has yet been built," he continued, "though the Baptists, Methodists and Episcopalians each have one ready to raise in a short time. Preaching is held in the railroad depot, and in the schoolhouses or 'academies' as they are called."

The Presbyterians in Atlanta that year—White counted three including himself—met with a nondenominational congregation in a log cabin that housed the Male Academy. Money for the structure had been raised early in 1847 by subscription, and it had been built in what one early writer called "a chinquapin thicket" in the triangle formed by Pryor, Houston, and Peachtree Streets. Rev. John Simpson Wilson, pastor of Decatur Presbyterian Church, inaugurated the services at the Academy, and he and ministers of other denominations took turns preaching.

By the dawn of 1848, there apparently were at least nineteen Presbyterians in Atlanta. That number, led by Dr. Wilson, organized their own congregation on January 8. An extract from a Declaration and Rules adopted by the members reads as follows:

We, therefore, whose names are hereunto subscribed, being by the Providence of God assembled in this place, and desiring to enjoy the benefits, privileges and ordinances of the Church of Christ, as received and administered in the Presbyterian Church in these United States, of which church we are all members and communicants, do agree to unite in the organization of a church to be known as "The Presbyterian Church of Atlanta."

Adopted and subscribed by us at Atlanta, this 8th January, 1848.

Joel Kelsey
O. Houston
James Davis
Minerva Kelsey
Mary A. Thompson
Jane Davis
Keziah Boyd
C.J. Caldwell
H.A. Fraser
Margaret Boyd
Mary J. Thompson
Julia M.L. Fraser
Annie L. Houston
Joseph Thompson
Lucinda Cone
Jane Gill
Henry Brockman
Harriet Norcross
Ruth A. Brockman

THE SHORTER
CATECHISM

OF THE

WESTMINSTER ASSEMBLY

———

STANDARD EDITION

———

PHILADELPHIA
PRESBYTERIAN BOARD OF PUBLICATION
AND SABBATH-SCHOOL WORK
1899

Among articles collected in the First Church archives is this Shorter Catechism, *published in 1899.*

Ruling elders of the congregation were Joel Kelsey, a railroad-car builder whom Franklin C. Talmage, author of *The Story of the Presbytery of Atlanta,* calls "an aggressive Presbyterian"; Oswald Houston, the first city treasurer and the man for whom Houston Street was named; and James Davis. Shortly after the church was formed, Alexander F. Luckie, a pioneer landowner for whom Luckie Street was named, also was elected a ruling elder.

For five years following organization of the Atlanta church, Dr. Wilson was stated supply, giving the congregation one Sunday each month for two years, and, beginning in 1850, two Sundays. Half of Dr. Wilson's time was given to the Atlantans, much to the chagrin of Decatur Presbyterians, according to Talmage. But Wilson, who had come to frontier Georgia as a twenty-five-year-old missionary in 1821, had been drawn toward the settlement that would be incorporated as Atlanta in 1847 almost from its beginning. "We have labored in this city since its foundation," he said in a sermon delivered in 1860, "having, so far as we know, been the first to preach the Gospel, while it was yet know as Terminus [1837–1842], before it was honored with the more dignified name of Marthasville [Terminus was renamed Marthasville in 1842 and was incorporated as such in 1843]."

᷈᷈

In 1850, the Atlanta Presbyterian Church began construction of a church building on a lot on Marietta Street near the corner of Spring Street that later became part of the site occupied by the Federal Reserve Bank. The lot, part of Land Lot 78, was given by church trustee Judge Reuben Cone (for whom Cone Street is named), whom journalist White described in 1847 as a "northern man and a Democrat" who owned "much property in Atlanta in unimproved lots" and the "handsomest" residence in the city, located on Marietta Street. According to Franklin M. Garrett, author of volumes one and two of *Atlanta and Environs,* and a member of First Church, Cone was one of the two original owners of the two basic land lots (202½ acres each), 77 and 78, on which Atlanta was built. Cone owned, Garrett said, "right smart of land, as the boys would say."

During 1850, 1851, and 1852, the church constructed a red brick building measuring seventy by forty feet at a cost of about forty-two hundred dollars. Described by Atlantan John Stainback Wilson (a physician and apparently no relation to Reverend Wilson) in his 1871

Atlanta As It Is as a "plain, neat building," the church had a pediment, cornices, and window casing of white, and was surrounded by a white picket fence. Over the vestibule of the main floor, reserved for worship, was a gallery for the organ and choir, and Sunday School classes were held in the "lecture room" in the basement. From 1855 to 1861, a weekday school called the Atlanta Select School also was held in the basement. The structure was topped with a square white belfry that was empty. No bell was ever installed, Garrett wrote in *Atlanta and Environs,* because John Silvey, whose house was nearby, went to bed at 7 P.M. and gave a "generous contribution in return for which it was agreed that there would be no bell to interrupt his early nocturnal rest."

The building was dedicated on July 4, 1852, with three services. Dr. Wilson preached at the morning service, during which fourteen new members were received; Dr. Robert C. Smith of the faculty of Oglethorpe University preached in the afternoon; and Rev. Remembrance Chamberlain, a Congregational Church minister who, like Wilson, had been a pioneer Georgian missionary, preached in the evening.

Between 1853 and 1858 the church was served by Rev. J.L. King, stated supply for ten months, and Rev. J.E. Dubose, stated supply for 1854 and pastor for the next three years. In 1858, the Presbyterian Church of Atlanta was divided into the First Presbyterian Church of Atlanta and the Second Presbyterian Church of Atlanta (later to be called the Central Presbyterian Church of Atlanta), and after the division, sixty-two-year-old Dr. Wilson was chosen pastor of First Church and served until his death in 1873.

According to Franklin Talmage, many crosscurrents were at work in the decision to divide the Presbyterian congregation of Atlanta, including unrest created by the widespread political activity of people advocating secession from the Union and the divergent views held by people coming to the city from "all sections of the nation, both north and south" at the rate of one thousand per year. A less amorphous reason was the objection of members to some of the "pew-holders" who purchased pews and attended the church, but did not join, yet "claimed a voice in affairs."

The Flint River Presbytery, established in 1834 (and from which the Atlanta Presbytery was carved in 1867), tried repeatedly to heal the breach in the Atlanta church, but failed, and in February 1858 decreed that two churches be formed, that the property be equitably

Dr. John Wilson

No Sound Save the Thunder's Roar

ew men in the present day know anything of the toil and suffering it required to lay the foundation of Presbyterianism in western Georgia," Dr. John Simpson Wilson, First Presbyterian Church's inaugural pastor, wrote after fifty years in the ministry. "It was a day of small things. The seed had to be sown, houses of worship erected, and the scattered sheep gathered. Churches which now contribute thousands to support their pastors and benevolent enterprises of the day were then but a mere handful, without wealth. . . . Hard work and hard fare was the allotment of all laborers in this part of the vineyard."

Twenty-five-year-old John Wilson and his young wife, Juliet Simpson Means Wilson, came to Georgia in 1821, at the beginning of a decade of western migration that brought one hundred thousand settlers into the state by ox cart and wagon, on foot, and on horseback. As the settlers built their first houses, most of them log cabins, they felt the need also to provide schools and churches. "Academies sprang up, presided over by learned men," Franklin C. Talmage wrote in *The Story of the Presbytery of Atlanta*.

"In many cases these learned men were ministers of the Gospel."

Wilson, one of those "learned men," first took up the task of preaching, teaching, and serving as a missionary in the settlement of Ruckersville, nearly due east of Atlanta and just over the border from his native South Carolina. Writing about the rigors of his work in frontier Georgia he said, "The week was spent in the school room and the Sabbath in the church. On Saturday I went to my field of labor, preaching at night, then preaching twice on Sabbath, and returned home on Sabbath night and was in the school room on Monday morning, often riding thirty miles amid darkness and solitude, having deep streams and dangerous bridges to cross, with no light save the lightning's glare, and no sound save the thunder's roar and the growl of the wolf."

In 1824, the Wilsons moved westward to the Presbyterian church at Lawrenceville, in Gwinnett County, and in 1844 they moved to the Decatur church, which Dr. Wilson helped organize. In 1859, Dr. Wilson became pastor of the Atlanta Presbyterian Church, which he had helped organize while he was pastor in Decatur.

"[Dr. Wilson] taught school nearly all of his ministerial life," James Stacy wrote in *A History of the Presbyterian Church in Georgia,* published in 1912, "never being released from the school room till his removal to Atlanta in 1859. When at Lawrenceville, he had a large attendance of young men, many of whom entered the ministry. . . . But he was especially useful in the ministry as a missionary, he having organized as many as fourteen churches."

During Dr. Wilson's ministry, according to Stacy, he served as a delegate to eleven General Assemblies and was moderator of the 1864 Assembly held in Charlotte.

He also was organizing moderator of the Flint River Presbytery (1835) and clerk of the Synod of Georgia from its organization in 1845 until 1872. Dr. Wilson, who in 1869 published *Necrology,* thirty-three sketches of deceased ministers of the Synod and a brief history of the Presbyterian Church in Georgia, was given an honorary Doctor of Divinity degree in 1852 by Oglethorpe University. He died in 1873, after fifty-two years of ministry.

According to Stacy, one of Dr. Wilson's friends once said of him, "I am sometimes tempted to be a little skeptical, but it all vanishes when I look at the grand old disciple, that living demonstration of Christianity."

divided, and that the church to be called the First Presbyterian Church of Atlanta retain the Marietta Street building.

On February 21, 1858, according to the earliest book of First Church session minutes, a meeting was held to organize the congregation, "the Atlanta Presbyterian Church having been divided." The minutes list 60 members, including ruling elders Joel Kelsey, A. (Alex) N. Wilson, George Robinson, B. (Berryman) D. Shumate, William Markham, and O. (Oswald) Houston.

During a March 1859 session meeting, the congregation was divided into four geographical districts, each of which an assigned elder was to visit regularly. By March 1860, the church counted 145 church members and 12 children in "Sabbath School and Bible Class," and in June of that year, Lavinia Cobb, a "colored woman" who came before the session, "was received into the communion of the church" after giving "satisfactory evidence of her faith in Christ."

As the church proceeded with its regular business in 1860, the nation outside its doors moved to the brink of war. On December 21, news reached Atlanta that South Carolina had seceded from the Union the previous day, and on the twenty-second, the city celebrated all day. "Salutes were fired in the morning," Franklin Talmage wrote, "and the day closed with a great torch-light parade. . . ."

During 1861, the year Georgia followed South Carolina in secession and the Confederacy fired on Fort Sumter, the session of First Church recorded six meetings, and during the following two war years, they met about once each month. One of the entries for 1863 notes that the church numbered 159 members, 80 children in Sabbath School and Bible Class, and 2 "colored communicants." During 1864, two meetings were recorded, in January and March. At the January meeting, reception of a third "colored communicant" was noted as follows: "Anthony servant of . . . appeared proffering a wish to become a member of the church. [After he was examined] he was admitted to membership." Neither the 1864 entries nor the others written during the war mention anything other than the specific business of the church. With the March 1864 entry, the record ends, to be taken up again September 17, 1865.

This 1902 bulletin shows First Church's second building, which was constructed on Marietta Street where the first building, the "old war church," once stood.

The First Presbyterian Church

ATLANTA, GEORGIA.

REV. C. P. BRIDEWELL, PASTOR.

RESIDENCE: 31 CONE STREET.

TELEPHONE No. 917 (BELL.)

The Pastor will be pleased to meet visitors and strangers after each service.

As the Civil War threatened to engulf Atlanta in the summer of 1864, many women, children, and older people left the city. Dr. Wilson, then sixty-eight, "escaped to the south," writes Talmage, "and then by a circuitous route reached South Carolina [his native state]. His manuscripts and library were shipped by freight car to South Carolina for safe-keeping. Unfortunately they were intercepted by enemy forces and all were burned. Among these papers were numerous historical sketches from which he as historiographer was to produce a history of Presbyterianism in the area."

During the Battle of Atlanta, which began in mid-July and ended when the city was surrendered to Gen. William Tecumseh Sherman September 1, Dr. Wilson's son, a physician, was shot down on a city street as he cared for the wounded, and a son of former pastor Rev. J.E. Dubose also was killed. While the city was under siege, the First Church building on Marietta Street "received half a dozen or more [shells], which at one time . . . drove out a number of citizens that had sought it as a place of refuge and safety," the *Atlanta Intelligentser* reported. The church escaped the torch, however, when General Sherman's troops burned most of the city in November, leaving it, John Stainback Wilson later wrote in *Atlanta As It Is*, "a fit habitation only for bats and for owls."

First Church pastor Dr. Wilson offered the following commentary: "The churches suffered greatly in the late war. . . . [The membership was] scattered and driven into exile, some of them dying, and others taking up their permanent abode in the regions to which they fled, . . . and those who did return [were] greatly impoverished and discouraged. For many months the exercises of religion were suspended in most of their churches. The effects of the storm of war that has passed over . . . cannot be contemplated without the most profound sorrow." Yet even as he chronicled the devastation, Wilson sounded a note of hope. "But the King in Zion lives," he wrote, "and will restore her breaches."

In the war's wake, Atlanta turned to the task of rebuilding. By 1866, First Church had repaired its damaged structure and that year allowed the basement to be used by the Atlanta Female Institute and College of Music. "As the cities and towns [of the Presbytery] rose from the ashes, so also builders began to rebuild Zion, and the shepherds began to gather the scattered sheep," Talmage wrote.

Six years after Sherman's departure, John Stainback Wilson reported the city much improved from the "apparently hopeless wreck" it was in the summer of 1865. "But how changed the scene in this year of grace, 1871!" he wrote. "[There is] a maze of new streets and building that have spread themselves far beyond the old city limits. . . ." (Any plan drawn up for the streets was, he said, all but nonexistent: "[The plan] . . . is about this: Where you find a road, take it.")

ҩ

In March 1873, Dr. Wilson died, and the following summer the church called Dr. Joseph H. Martin to be its pastor. About two thousand dollars was subsequently spent in repairing, renovating, and improving the church building, but by 1876 members felt the need for a new building. The congregation had outgrown the first building, according to a short history in the 1883 church directory, and the structure showed the "decay of age and the effects of war and the elements." In late 1876 and early 1877, plans were solidified for a new structure on the same site, and W.C. Smith, who was the architect for buildings at Vanderbilt University, was employed. On July 17, 1877, a contract was let for the Gothic-style church, estimated to cost about thirty-five thousand dollars, including the expense of tearing down the old church. (The final cost was recorded as being $36,422.97.) Until the building was completed in October 1879, the First Church congregation met at the Methodist Episcopal Church on Marietta Street.

In January 1883, after the fall 1882 resignation of Reverend Martin, the church called Dr. E.H. Barnett, a native of Virginia, who as a captain in the Army of the Confederacy fought in Georgia and was one of the last soldiers to leave Atlanta when it was evacuated. Called from the pastorate of the Presbyterian church in Abingdon, Virginia, Dr. Barnett was installed in June.

In all probability, when Dr. Barnett arrived he saw a city similar to that Louise Black MacDougald described in "A Trip Down Peachtree in 1886," published in the *Atlanta Historical Bulletin* in April 1940. Traveling from Union Depot toward her grandparents' house at Peachtree and Fourth Streets, she first saw retail businesses, "offices of famous men," and "many saloons." At Ellis Street, the businesses (except for two grocery stores) gave way "to homes of most of the Four Hundred of Atlanta." Around the homes, she wrote, "almost all the grass planted in the front and back lawns was surrounded with fences for protection against loose animals and mad dogs. There were no cattle laws. Farmers from the country would continually bring in herds of cows, flocks of sheep and droves of hogs for market, driving them down the middle of streets, and especially this one, it seemed."

If her trip had been in mid-summer and not mid-December, she wrote, "the people would have been rocking in rocking-chairs on the porches, waving to us as we passed. . . . And any who may have been walking on the dusty sidewalks would have been dressed in the fashion of the day. The women in long sleeved, high-neck, corseted, basque fitted costumes . . . The men in high cut, vested suits with shirts having starched wing collars. Bonnet hats on the women, tied under the chin. And the men in black derbies."

During his fifteen years as pastor of First Church, Dr. Barnett, a scholar of the Greek and Hebrew languages, helped establish the Barnett Mission (later Barnett Memorial Presbyterian Church) near the Exposition Mills, and he is said to have refused a one-thousand-dollar raise at one point, saying he would prefer the money be used for charity and the work of the church.

At Dr. Barnett's death in September 1898, Dr. Richard O. Flinn was stated supply until May 1899, when some 120 First Church members withdrew and formed North Avenue Presbyterian Church under his leadership. Rev. C.P. Bridewell then served as pastor until 1906, Dr. Walter L. Lingle until 1911 (when

he left to serve on the faculty of Union Theological Seminary in Richmond and later was appointed president of Davidson College), and Rev. Hugh K. Walker until May 1914. Dr. J. Sprole Lyons came as pastor in June 1914 with the intention of helping the church realize its long-delayed plans to move from Marietta Street to a more residential location.

Such a move had been contemplated as early as 1910, when it was suggested that the church sell its Marietta Street lot and buy property at the junction of Peachtree and West Peachtree near Baker Street, then available for $40,000. No decision was made, however, and six months later, the price of the lot had been raised to $75,000. Two years later, the congregation authorized the Board of Trustees to buy the "vacant lot" at the northwest corner of Peachtree and Sixteenth Streets from S.M. Inman, chairman of the board. The cost of the property (162 feet on Peachtree, running back 251 feet on Sixteenth) was just under $50,000.

After four distinct plans for acquiring the money were proposed and rejected in 1913, a fifth plan was proposed by which funds would be raised through subscriptions from church members. Led by the vision of Mr. Inman, the Building Committee accepted the fifth plan in April 1914, and six weeks later the money had been subscribed. In addition to these funds, the sale of the Marietta Street site had brought $102,500.

On May 21, 1914, the trustees turned to the matter of the structure itself and limited expenditures for a sanctuary and Sunday School building to $75,000, not including organ and furniture. Building plans were put on hold, however, on September 2, because of "unsettled business conditions," according to the minutes. At a subsequent meeting, on September 21, Dr. Lyons, who had met with the committee for the first time in late June, "spoke at some length," urging that they proceed at once with the erection of the "Sunday School Room." His position was supported by other committee members, and "by unanimous consent, it was decided to build at once the Sunday School part of the plant. . . ."

Four years after the initial efforts to move, First Church was on its way to Peachtree.

Chapter III

The Church in a World at War

"[On Christmas Day] several of the churches held morning services, others in the evening. Here were voiced prayer after prayer for the soldiers, for the country, for the victory of America and for a speedy peace. . . ."
— The Atlanta Journal
December 25, 1917

Atlanta, Ga. - April 10th, 1914.

Whereas, Mr. S. M. Inman, upon the request of the Officers and members of the First Presbyterian Church of Atlanta, is carrying for the said church a certain lot on Peachtree Road, and

Whereas, the indebtedness due to Mr. Inman on the said lot is approximately fifty thousand dollars ($50,000.00) and it is desired to pay off the indebtedness and for the First Presbyterian Church of Atlanta to acquire title to the said lot,

Now, Therefore (We the undersigned subscribers agree to pay to the First Presbyterian Church of Atlanta the sums set opposite our names, upon the following conditions, to-wit:-

First - That the sums so subscribed shall be used for the payment of the said lot on Peachtree Road.

Second - That the surplus, if any, be used on improvements on the said lot.

Third - These subscriptions to be binding only when the sums subscribed herein below shall equal the sum of fifty thousand dollars ($50,000.00) provided also that

(Ford)

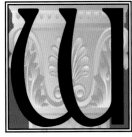

hen eight-year-old Franklin Garrett arrived in Atlanta from Chicago with his parents in May 1914, the family soon found a house on Thirteenth Street between Piedmont Road and Peachtree Street. The area was quiet, nearly all residential, although there were a few privately owned neighborhood grocery and drug stores at Peachtree and Tenth Streets. "It was a very desirable part of town in which to live," Garrett remembers.

It was to this bucolic neighborhood that members of First Church came on December 31, 1914, to break ground for their new Sunday School building. "Quite a large company of people were present at this ceremony," according to a church historian of the time. Elder William Bensel, the oldest member of the congregation, was invited to turn the first spadeful of ground at the vacant lot. In the months that followed, "Under Dr. Lyons' leadership the work of erecting the new church went forward untiringly," the historian wrote, and the building was ready for occupancy less than a year later.

On December 5, 1915, the congregation gathered in the main Sunday School room, which had been furnished with the walnut pews and pulpit from the Marietta Street church, and there Dr. J. Sprole Lyons preached the first sermon at the new location. That same month, Ellen Marian Fleming, daughter of Mr. and Mrs. Paul L. Fleming, became the first infant baptized in the church on Peachtree.

Left: This 1914 note in a church ledger formalizes the terms of the purchase from Elder Samuel M. Inman of the Peachtree lot on which the new First Church was built.

Preceding page: The Cradle Roll Class of 1925 sent this picture to their mothers on Mother's Day. The child at the far right is little Eleanor Hoyt, who is now Eleanor Dabney.

THE B. L. HEARN COMPANY
REAL ESTATE AND COMMISSION MERCHANTS

ATLANTA PHONE 5726-A
110 ELM STREET

ATLANTA, GA., *Aug 12, 1916*

Mr. G. H. Harrison,
Atlanta,
Ga.

Dear Sir,

Please write me the lowest price the church will take for that lot and if I can not get any more I will sell it. I have been laid up since last Friday again.

Answer me quick. I have a combination form to buy the church.

Yours sincerely,

B. L. Hearn

P.S.

Must I accept the organ and benches in making the sale? or not?

B. L. H.

Above: On August 12, 1916, real estate broker B.L. Hearn urged a swift end to negotiations to sell the First Church property on Marietta Street. His letter was addressed to church Elder George W. Harrison.

Opposite: When little Miss Louise Richardson was promoted from the Cradle Roll Department in 1921, she received this certificate. Miss Richardson later married Ivan Allen Jr., who was elected mayor of Atlanta in 1961.

As First Church convened at its Peachtree location, the Sunday School enrollment was 355, with 41 officers and teachers, 300 "scholars," and 14 children in the Cradle Roll. One of the new Cradle Roll members was little Caroline Paullin. Caroline, who later would marry Dr. William R. Minnich, was the daughter of Dr. and Mrs. James Edgar Paullin, who lived on Fifteenth Street. At age three, she had not previously been to Sunday School because there was no provision for very young children. At home, however, she had been taught about the Bible. "I had a wonderful Negro mammy who loved the church," she said. "She couldn't read, but there were a lot of pictures in her Bible, and I knew it from start to finish with Mammy's interpretation of the pictures. Later, Mammy took me to Sunday School. We just walked there, as did many children in our neighborhood."

Eleanor Hoyt Dabney also remembers being "dressed to the nines" and taken to Sunday School by her nurse in the mid-1920s, and she remembers that she was taught by Miss Blanche Heywood in the nursery class. "As I remember, there were fifteen or twenty nurses," said Dabney, whose great-grandfather, S.B. Hoyt, was an elder in the church during the Civil War. Mrs. Dabney also remembers a class was

34

MADONNA BY N. SICHEL

PROMOTION CERTIFICATE

This Certifies

That *Louise Richardson*

Is Transferred from the Cradle Roll to the

Beginners Department

of the *First Presbyterian* Sunday School

of *Atlanta Georgia*

Blanche Heywood
Supt. Cradle Roll Dept.

Sam S. Heynen
Supt. Sunday School

Dated *Sept 25* 19*21*   *J. Sprole Lyons*
Pastor

Dr. J. Sprole Lyons

In his short history of First Church, the late George B. Hoyt, an elder, wrote: "By 1914, the territory surrounding [the church building on Marietta Street] had become all business and it was necessary to move to a new location. The church was decreasing in numbers and in usefulness, so Dr. J. Sprole Lyons came to be pastor with the avowed purpose of moving the church. . . . The [Peachtree] site was selected and [buildings] erected. Not a member was lost from the church roll in this move and the church immediately began to grow again. . . . Dr. Lyons was one of the strong leaders of the entire Southern Presbyterian Church," Hoyt continued. "He was very meticulous in dress and manner, preached strong exegetical sermons, and had a great gift as an organizer."

Born in Tazewell, Virginia, in 1861, J. Sprole Lyons followed in the footsteps of his father, Rev. Jonathan L. Lyons, preparing for the Presbyterian ministry at King College in Bristol, Tennessee, and at Union Theological Seminary in Richmond, Virginia. Prior to his move to Atlanta, he had served churches in Lawrenceburg, Kentucky (seven years); Mt. Sterling, Kentucky (one year); San Antonio, Texas (one year); and Louisville, Kentucky (twenty-two years).

During his ministry, he served the Presbyterian Church in many capacities, including moderator of the synods of Kentucky and Georgia and the General Assembly, member of the Executive Committee of Home Missions, and trustee of Agnes Scott College, Columbia Theological Seminary, Presbyterian College, and Rabun Gap-Nacoochee School. He was awarded three honorary doctorates, from the Central University of Kentucky, Princeton University, and King College.

When Dr. Lyons died in 1942, a colleague, Reverend Henry H. Sweets, quoted a professor of homiletics at the Kentucky Presbyterian Seminary in

Louisville, who told his students during Lyons's pastorate in that city: "I am glad to tell you that we have here in Louisville in the person of Dr. J.S. Lyons the finest exponent of expository preaching of whom I know."

"He was a wonderful person and pastor," said lifelong First Church member Mamie Lowe Hubbard, "and a marvelous preacher."

On April 6, 1919, under the pastorate of Dr. J. Sprole Lyons, First Church celebrated completion of its Peachtree sanctuary.

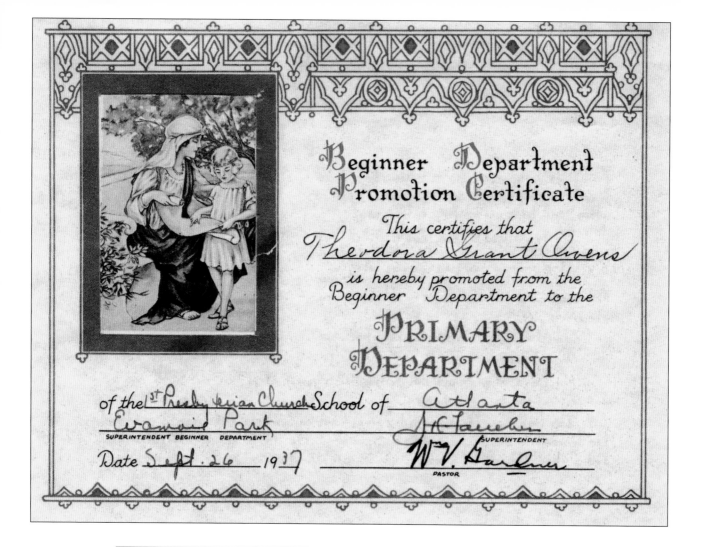

Beginner Department Promotion Certificate

This certifies that

Theodora Grant Owens

is hereby promoted from the
Beginner Department to the

PRIMARY DEPARTMENT

of the 1st Presbyterian Church School of _Atlanta_

Evamoil Park

SUPERINTENDENT BEGINNER DEPARTMENT

SUPERINTENDENT

Date _Sept. 26_ 19_37_

PASTOR

Little Miss Theodora Grant Owens (Mrs. "Dodie" Chapman) received this certificate of promotion from the Beginner Department to the Primary Department.

Opposite: This letter of appreciation was sent to church Elder George W. Harrison shortly after the Marietta Street property was sold. Elder Harrison had worked arduously to complete the details of the sale.

formed for the nurses, after which they met for their own Sunday School lesson in a room next to the children.

As Caroline Minnich (née Paullin) was being introduced to Sunday School in 1915 in her quiet Peachtree neighborhood, troubling news was coming from Europe, where Britain and France and their allies were at war with Germany and its allies. As the hostilities widened, America's participation began to seem inevitable, and in 1917, as First Church made plans to build its Peachtree sanctuary, President Woodrow Wilson signed a declaration of war against Germany.

Many Atlantans responded to the declaration by joining the armed forces,

BROWN & RANDOLPH, PARKER & SCOTT

LAWYERS

EDWARD T. BROWN
HOLLINS N. RANDOLPH
ROBERT S. PARKER
HUGH M. SCOTT

CABLE ADDRESS "BROWNRAN"

210-219 BROWN-RANDOLPH BUILDING

ATLANTA, GA.

January 1, 1917.

Mr. George W. Harrison,
    Atlanta, Georgia.
Dear Mr. Harrison:

      The consummation of the sale by The First
Presbyterian Church of Atlanta to The Federal Reserve Bank of
Atlanta of the Marietta Street lot having been effected,we desire to express our appreciation of the untiring energy shown
by you in arranging the details incident to closing this trans-
action. Your services have been invaluable to the Church and
of great assistance to us in putting the matter in final shape.
It must be a considerable source of satisfaction to you to have
so largely aided in rendering merchantable the Church titles.

      We understand that it has always been a
tradition in your wife's family that Judge Cone gave this property to The First Presbyterian Church of Atlanta in the days
of it's infancy. It has remained for you and the descendants
of Judge Cone to render the service which has enabled the Church
to reap the full return from this gift.

      Very truly yours,

H. N. Randolph
R. S. Parker

RSP-A

39

jamming recruiting offices "anxious to get into uniform," Franklin Garret wrote in *Atlanta and Environs,* and at

---

At a December 7, 1913, Congregational Meeting, First Church members authorized the Trustees to sell the Marietta Street church and to use the funds to build a "Church and Sunday School Building" at Peachtree and Sixteenth Streets.

Fort McPherson, where many recruits would be trained, "tents sprung up in the grounds like vegetables in a rich garden." In June, the War Department announced that Atlanta would get an additional camp (Camp John B. Gordon), to be located in the Cross Keys District of DeKalb County.

Atlanta's first Christmas at war since 1864 found thousands of soldiers in the area, many of whom spent Christmas Eve and Christmas Day in the city, staying in hotels, with families, and at the YMCA. "[On Christmas Day] several of the churches held morning services, others in the evening," the *Journal* reported. "Here were voiced prayer after prayer for the soldiers, for the country, for the victory of America and for a speedy peace. . . ."

The peace Americans prayed for came the following year, when Germany signed an armistice agreement at daybreak on November 11, 1918. During the first war to involve most of the civilized world, tens of thousands of Americans were killed in battle and hundreds of thousands more had been wounded or were dead of

MEMORANDA
In Re
The First Presbyterian Church,   Atlanta.

- - - -

Dec. 7, 1913, the Congregation authorized The Board of Trustees to sell the Marietta St. church property and improve the Peachtree and 16th Sts. property, purchased of Mr. S. M. Inman, fronting 162 ft. on Peachtree and extending back 251 feet on Sixteenth St., which lot cost the Church $54,117.60. Of this amount, $50,000.00 was raised by special collection from the congregation, the balance, viz: $4,117.60, was paid out of proceeds of the sale of the Marietta St. church property to The FEDERAL RESERVE BANK OF ATLANTA on Wednesday, Dec. 27th 1916, for $102,500.00 cash.

BUILDING COMMITTEE.
The First Presbyterian Church, Atlanta, Ga.

S. W. Carson, Chairman,
Geo. W. Harrison, Secretary,
E. P. Ansley,   Chas. R. Winship, John J. Woodside,
W. R. Hoyt,   Elected Sept. 2, 1914.
S. M. Inman, Honorary and Advisory,
Wm. Bensel, Honorary,
James W. English, Honorary,
Frank M. Inman, Honorary, elected upon death of his father Mr. S. M. Inman,

W. T. Downing)
E. C. Wachendorff) Architects.

Sunday, Aug. 19th 1917.
The Pastor, Dr. J. Sprole Lyons, announced the following Committee on laying corner stone:
Chmn.
Geo. W. Harrison) From
W. R. Hoyt   ) The Session

Paul L. Fleming, Superintendent of Sunday School,
Gilham H. Morrow, Chairman Board of Deacons,
S. W. Carson, Chairman The Building Committee,
Judge W. T. Newman, Chairman The Board of Trustees

other war-related causes. Atlantans celebrated the end of World War I on November 12 with a parade of more than ten thousand troops and thousands of civilians.

During 1919, Atlanta began to rediscover its social inclinations. That year, the Metropolitan Opera Company brought Enrico Caruso and his bride to the city, and social calendars filled with debutante parties, tea dances, and balls. "High fashion for femininity," a local newspaper reported, "called for skirts touching high-topped laced or button shoes for daytime, and extremely pointed pumps ornamented with big buckles for afternoon wear. . . . Hats embroidered in gold and silver threads, pocketbooks suspended from bracelets and satin dresses were all the rage."

"Those were grand times," said Mrs. Rebecca Young Frazer, a First Church member whose father, H. Lane Young, and husband, James N. Frazer, each served for years as chairman of the church's board of trustees. "I remember watching my parents leave for social occasions, and seeing the wonderful clothes they wore. Many of the people who entertained owned large estates, and many, such as Mr. and Mrs. John W. Grant [whose home is now Cherokee Town Club on West Paces Ferry Road] and Mr. and Mrs. Edward Inman [who built the Swan House, now part of the Atlanta History Center], were member of First Church.

"Many church members lived in the beautiful homes that lined Peachtree, people such as Mrs. Joseph M. High, who gave the land upon which the High Museum was built. I remember seeing Mrs. High and her daughter [Mrs. D.R. Peteet] walking to church. Those were days of elegance," Mrs. Frazer said. "It was more like living in the Victorian Era than the twentieth century."

But not all Atlantans moved in those circles. At the end of World War I, many people led simple, hard lives, keeping cows and chickens, tending gardens, heating their homes with wood stoves, bathing in washtubs on Saturday nights, and using outdoor toilets. Vendors sold chickens, fruit, and vegetables on the streets.

In the spring following the war, First Church celebrated completion of its new English Gothic sanctuary, construction of which had officially begun with the laying of a cornerstone in October 1917. Dedicated on April 6, 1919, in a service conducted by Dr. Lyons, the sanctuary measured approximately seventy-seven feet by eighty-six feet. The ceiling of the

hen Dr. J. Sprole Lyons retired in 1936 as pastor of First Church, a young man named William V. Gardner was called. "Dr. Lyons took him as his spiritual son," a church historian wrote, "and the beautiful relationship between them was an inspiration."

Dr. Gardner, who was born in Saltillo, Mississippi, in 1903, received the bachelor and master of divinity degrees from Union Theological Seminary of Virginia, Richmond, in 1928 and 1930, and the doctor of theology degree from Presbyterian College in 1937. Before coming to Atlanta, he served Presbyterian churches in Tuscumbia, Alabama (1930–1933), and Farmville, Virginia (1933–1936). During his pastorate at First Church, he was named chairman of the Board of Trustees of Columbia Seminary, a member of the Board of

Dr. William V. Gardner

Trustees of Agnes Scott College, and chairman of the Executive Committee of Home Missions of the Presbyterian Church U.S.

First Church member Rosalie Parris, director of the weekday kindergarten for many years, remembers that Dr. Gardner visited the children two or three times each week. "He would go out in the yard and play with them," she said, his tall body looming over them, his large hands helping them in their games. "When he raised his hand for the benediction," recalled a long-time church member, "you really felt blessed."

Gardner, who led First Church through the difficult days of World War II, displayed his gentleness one Sunday when an older member rose from her seat in the middle of his sermon and began to berate the congregation. When the woman paused, Dr. Gardner quickly but kindly said, "Thank you," calling her by name. "Now will the congregation please rise for the benediction."

In 1922, the Atlanta Presbytery began holding conferences for children, youth, and adults at Camp Smyrna. Among the attendees at a 1940s conference were Dr. William V. Gardner, Fraser Hart, Ben Dunn, Jane Jones, and Billie Parigna.

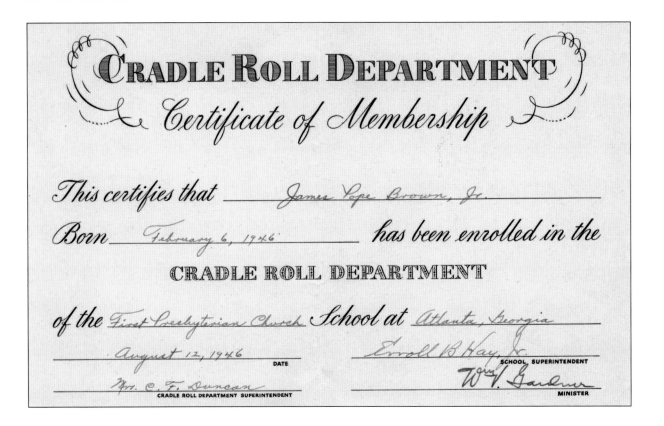

CRADLE ROLL DEPARTMENT
Certificate of Membership

This certifies that _James Pope Brown, Jr._

Born _February 6, 1946_ has been enrolled in the

CRADLE ROLL DEPARTMENT

of the _First Presbyterian Church_ School at _Atlanta, Georgia_

August 12, 1946 DATE

Erroll B Hay, Jr. SCHOOL SUPERINTENDENT

Mrs. C. F. Duncan CRADLE ROLL DEPARTMENT SUPERINTENDENT

Wm V. Gardner MINISTER

Above: When children are born, they become members of the Cradle Roll Department.

Below: Miss Mamie Heinz, founder of the First Church Day Kindergarten, was a much sought-after consultant in early childhood education well into her eighties

room, which reached a height of sixty feet in the center, was ornamented with molded and pierced truss work of wood stained a warm brown color, and the plaster walls were "finished in a rough facing of a light cream tint, the rough facing being used to aid the acoustics," a church historian of the time wrote. The vestibule and aisles had been floored with Moravian tiles, and over the aisles were placed brown velvet runners to muffle the sound of entering feet. A new Pilcher organ, designed by church organist Charles A. Sheldon, had been installed in the sanctuary, and there were eleven large window spaces waiting for stained-glass windows. The *Christian Observer* called the interior "beautiful in the extreme, . . . deriving its chief charm for the simplicity of the idea."

In addition to seeing the fruition of efforts to complete the new buildings at Peachtree and Sixteenth, First Church saw in 1919 the fulfillment of another effort. It began with what Franklin Talmage called "a small struggling Sunday School at Peachtree Heights, which had been in operation for several years and was led by some [First Church] members." In the fall of 1919, Peachtree Heights Mission was organized as Peachtree Road Presbyterian Church, which would eventually become the largest Presbyterian church in America.

Above: In 1950, Mrs. Rosalie Parris (center) succeeded Miss Mamie Heinz as director of the Day Kindergarten and served until her retirement in 1974.

Below: In the 1930s, this greeting was sent from the Cradle Roll Department to children on their first birthday.

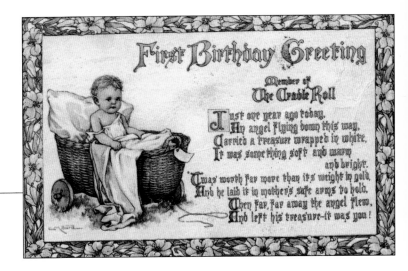

The inaugural class of Miss Mamie Heinz's weekday kindergarten, begun in 1946. At the front of the class, Charles Lockwood plays with a train.

The Peachtree Heights Mission had been one of a number organized by the members and pastors of First Church since the late 1800s, when Presbyterians began reaching out to various parts of the expanding city. Among the churches and missions First Church helped organize and support financially before 1919 had been Third Presbyterian Church, organized in 1874, whose name was changed to Moore Memorial in 1891; a Union Sunday School directed by Elder G.B. McGaughey, out of which grew West End Presbyterian Church, organized in 1887; the Barnett Mission, which became Barnett Memorial Church in 1890; and North Avenue Presbyterian Church, organized in 1898. The churches First Church helped found and support after 1919 were Morningside Presbyterian, organized in 1925; and Trinity Presbyterian, actively led in its formation by First Church pastor Dr. William V. Gardner, Dr. Lyons's successor, and established in 1949. Rev. Allison Williams, who grew up in First Church, became the founding minister of Trinity Presbyterian, and remained there forty years.

A faithful worker in First Church's mission endeavors was Arlene Peffer, who came to Atlanta in 1915 from Louisville, Kentucky, to be Dr. Lyons's secretary. Miss Peffer worked in the Barnett Mission and in the Bellwood Mission, begun in the 1930s by young parishioners of First Church. Bellwood was extant until 1953, when it was discontinued.

In the early 1920s, First Church forged a historic alliance with what would become another Atlanta institution, the city's first radio station, fledgling WSB.

"To Dr. Lyons should be given credit for foresight in the use of radio in worship," Franklin Talmage wrote of the pioneering broadcast. His reference is to the inauguration of WSB radio's airing of the First Church Sunday worship service, which took place on April 2, 1922. There had been great excitement in Atlanta when WSB, owned by the *Atlanta Journal,* went on the air the preceding month. "Atlanta is on the wireless map of the world," the *Journal* reported, with "the first inland commercial radio station in the South. . . . [The station] is preparing to receive and send what is called entertainment—music, singing, lectures and the like."

In preparation for the inauguration of the station, WSB officials had looked for a church whose worship service could be aired. "One after-

Miss Arlene Peffer, who served as secretary to Dr. J. Sprole Lyons, was for many years a tireless worker in the mission activities of First Church. Miss Peffer, wrote church historian Mary Doom, "had an amazing memory. No matter what you asked her, she would respond with complete information."

47

Dr. J. Sprole Lyons (left), his son Bill Lyons, and grandson Bill Lyons Jr.

Opposite: In this early picture of the sanctuary, the Abrahamic (left) and Advent windows had been installed and the room was being heated by radiators running along the walls. The blank window space in the middle later was filled with the window called The Law, The Psalms, The Prophets.

another turned us down, certain that the microphone would distract the worshipers and the broadcast would tempt them to stay home," an official said. "But First Presbyterian's Dr. J. Sprole Lyons believed otherwise." Unworried about distraction, Lyons foresaw comfort in at-home church services, both for listeners and for himself. Listeners, he said, "could go to sleep if they wanted to without disturbing me in the slightest—I couldn't see them!" According to the *Journal,* Lyons, as a result, delivered "the first sermon ever preached in the South by wireless." Today, First Church's broadcast is the longest continually operated radio ministry in America.

Besides coming to Atlanta homes, the inaugural broadcast of the First Church service was aired at Piedmont Park, where, the newspaper reported, it "was heard by throngs." Although Dr. Lyons's sermon was only partially understood because of static, "hymns and other musical features . . . came through the ether so clearly and distinctly that the listeners . . . easily recognized the familiar tunes."

In a 1973 sermon, Dr. Harry Fifield, who served First Church as pastor from 1953 to 1976, spoke of the

Winship Memorial Chapel Dedication

First Presbyterian Church
Atlanta Georgia
July 15, 1931

On July 15, 1931, the church dedicated Winship Memorial Chapel, given in memory of Elder Charles R. Winship.

Opposite: A children's choir sings at Easter in Winship Chapel. In 1965, the gold-colored panes behind the children were replaced by a stained-glass window depicting Christ and his parables. The window was given in memory of Elder Charles R. Winship and his wife, Ida Atkins Winship.

value of the broadcast ministry. "Letters, phone calls, and visits tell us to lives changed, faith enforced, at least one suicide thwarted as a result of this broadcast," he said. "A pilot listening at thirty thousand feet called later to say, 'Your text last Sunday was, "Lo, I am with you always." I suddenly realized He was with me, right there in the cockpit. I've neglected Him for a long time. I called to tell you I'm going back to my church next Sunday.'"

By 1928, the First Church Sunday School had grown so much in its new location that members planned to build additional rooms and to complete the tower on Peachtree left unfinished in the earlier sanctuary construction. Completed in December 1929, the addition housed a kitchen, dining room, choir room, and pastor's office and study, and rooms for the Cradle Roll, Beginners Class, Mothers' Class, Nurses' Class, Young People's Department, Primary Department, and Berean Class. (The Berean Class had been organized in 1914 as a successor to the Brotherhood Class, its biblical name having been suggested by Dr. Lyons.)

Further enhancing facilities at the new location were a fifteen-bell carillon given in 1930 by E.P. McBurney in memory of his father and mother, James C. and Lucinda M. McBurney, and Winship Memorial Chapel, giving in 1931 by Ida Atkins Winship, in memory

THE FUTURE BELONGS TO THOSE WHO PREPARE FOR IT

FIRST PRESBYTERIAN CHURCH CENTENNIAL EXPANSION CAMPAIGN

In a campaign coinciding with its 100th birthday, First Church raised funds for several goals, including the expansion of its Sunday School facilities, endowment of Presbyterian College, and establishment by the Presbytery of a new church in north Atlanta.

of her husband, church elder Charles R. Winship. In 1994, the McBurney bells were expanded into a four-octave, thirteen-ton carillon given in memory of Devereaux McClatchey III.

In 1934, in the first such list of the ongoing church history, the historian recorded that the 1,727 members of First Church were helping support nine foreign missionaries working in China, Korea, Mexico, Brazil, and Africa, and three home missionaries working in Georgia. Youth activities besides Sunday School that year included the Young People's League and Senior League, the Junior Choir, and Boy Scout Troop 60, which was founded in October 1924 and today is the oldest continually registered troop in the city. The women's group was the Women's Auxiliary, a body that had been authorized in 1912 by the General Assembly in an effort to strengthen and focus women's work. Prior to 1912, women's work had been ongoing, but its directions had largely been determined by leaders in individual churches.

In the spring of 1936, Dr. Lyons, having served as pastor for twenty-two years, resigned active leadership and by congregation action was made Pastor Emeritus. On April 19, Dr. William V. Gardner, thirty-two-year-old pastor of the Presbyterian Church of Farmville, Virginia, filled the pulpit as guest speaker, and several weeks later was called to First Church by unanimous vote of the congregation. To Dr. Gardner would fall the task of leading the church through another world war.

The area of Peachtree around Sixteenth Street was still mostly residential at the beginning of World War II, and First Church was still a neighborhood church. Moreover, Atlanta itself maintained its small-town ways. Ruth Norris Pratt, who came to Atlanta with her parents in 1919, and whose father, Lawrence M. Norris, served as First Church elder, laughs when recalling that in the days prior to the war many women who made purchases in stores told the clerks, "Just charge it to Papa."

Prior to the war, families still went home after church to large Sunday dinners of roast or chicken and ice cream made in a hand-turned freezer on a shady spot on the back porch.

World War II was set in motion on September 1, 1939, when Germany invaded Poland, and ended six years later nearly to the day. After the invasion of Poland, England and France demanded that Germany withdraw its troops and then declared war when Germany refused to do so. As both sides were joined by allies, the war widened, and in December 1941, following the attack on Pearl Harbor, the United States joined Britain and its allies in war against Japan, Germany, and Italy.

At First Church, members "were encouraged to take soldiers in the city home to lunch on Sunday," Eleanor Dabney said. "A lot of the soldiers came to our church, and we had a lot of our members in uniform somewhere else." The war years were an anxious time, Dabney said. "I can't express the fear that we felt, how real it was. And how people were willing to do whatever they had to do to face whatever we had coming. Put up with any shortage. Put up with any discomfort or any inconvenience."

On June 6, 1944, the United States and its allies began an invasion of Normandy at daybreak as a first step toward liberating France, by then occupied by German troops, and fighting their way toward Germany. The first eyewitness broadcast of the Normandy Invasion, Harold H. Martin recorded in Volume III of *Atlanta and Environs,* was written by *Atlanta Journal* Editor Wright Bryan and aired on WSB. "His opening words: 'In the first hour of D-day, the first spearhead of Allied Forces for the liberation of Europe landed by parachute in Northern France. . . . The Battle of Europe has begun, and our nation has delivered the first foot soldiers to this scene of action.'"

"As First Church members realized that an Allied invasion was imminent," Dabney said, "Dr. Gardner announced a prayer service for the evening of D-Day, whenever it came. We had been told, 'Whenever it happens, come.' [On the evening of June 6], we held the service in the

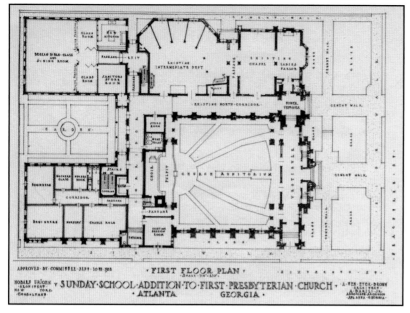

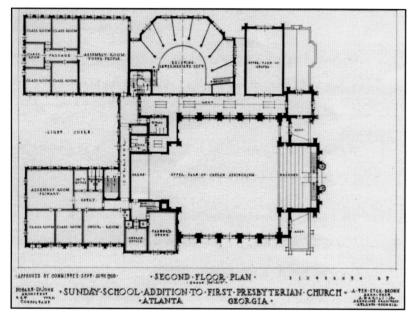

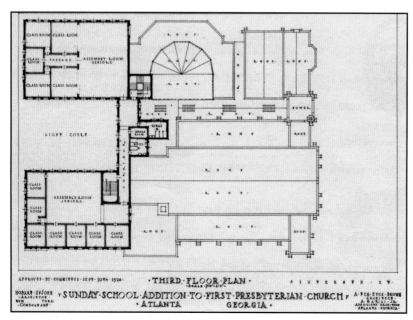

An expansion program completed in 1929 added space to First Church Sunday School facilities and completed the church tower.

old Pioneer room, and it was a most impressive, moving service, coming at a time when we didn't know what else we could do for the many sons from our church who were involved. We were frightened for them and frightened because we didn't know whether the invasion would succeed or fail. We just didn't have any idea. We knew our own country could be taken over if it failed. The room was packed, and we all felt very close to each other that night."

By August 15, 1944, German troops in France were in retreat, and on August 25, Paris was liberated. In March 1945, Americans crossed the Rhine, and on May 8, President Harry S. Truman announced that Germany had surrendered the day before. On August 15, 1945, Japan surrendered and the war was over.

That same day, a church historian wrote, "Dr. Gardner [conducted] the Victory Service at the church, in which thanks were given for our deliverance from World War II and pledges made for the rededication of our lives to the service of Christ." The historian

recorded the names of 281 First Church men and women who had served in the war, eleven whose lives were lost, and three who had been taken prisoner. During the first year after the war, the women of the church sent three tons of food and clothing to war-torn Europe.

In the fall of 1976, First Church became the first Presbyterian church in America to hold a weekday kindergarten for children, a program still in existence. The kindergarten was initiated by Mamie Heinz, a member of the church who also had originated the Beginners Class in the Marietta Street church. Miss Heinz was well known as an educator both in Atlanta and nationally. "Anybody whose life was touched by her became different," said Rosalie Parris, a church member who began teaching in the kindergarten in 1947 and stayed twenty-seven years. "She was a wonderful Christian. She lived her Christianity." When Miss Heinz retired in 1950, Mrs. Parris became director, and she served until her own retirement in 1974.

In 1947, First Church called Dr. J. Davison Philips as assistant pastor to help carry on the increasing number of church activities. (Dr. Philips later served as president of Columbia Seminary.) By 1948, the year of the church's Centennial,

When this photograph was taken, the trolley still ran down the middle of Peachtree Street and stopped in front of First Church at the corner of Sixteenth.

the staff numbered ten. Among the programs presented during the year-long Centennial celebration was a choir concert dedicated to members who had lost their lives in World War II, including Brooks Sheldon, the son of organist Charles Sheldon.

When Dr. Philips left in 1950, Rev. A. Allen Gardner became the church's assistant pastor, and he subsequently served as interim pastor from 1952 to 1953, after Dr. William Gardner's resignation.

In 1953, Dr. Harry A. Fifield, pastor of Westminster Presbyterian Church in Lynchburg, Virginia, was called as senior pastor. For the text of his first sermon, preached on Mother's Day, May 10, Dr. Fifield chose Isaiah 6:1–8, which ends: "And I heard the voice of the Lord, saying, Whom shall I send, and who will go for us? Then said I, Here am I; send me."

Dr. J. Davison Philips, former president of Columbia Theological Seminary, has long been a beloved figure at First Church. He is shown in this early picture with his wife, Kay, and young son, Jim.

Chapter IV

The Church in a Changing World

"What comes charging out of the past is the call to be love-in-action. Jesus was and is love-in-action. The heart of the Gospel is not a rule of safety, but an adventure of the spirit."

—Rev. Robert W. Bevis

For many years, the radiant faces of twin sisters with biblical names have been familiar to First Church members. Naomi Byrd and Ruth Law joined the church in 1947 and 1951, respectively, and both taught Sunday School for many years. In 1962, Naomi went to work at the church, and she has been there ever since, as staff secretary to six pastors and now volunteer secretary to a seventh, Dr. Ernest W. Davis, associate pastor for Church Growth. Ruth has been a bookkeeping volunteer at First Church since 1975, when she retired after many years as an executive secretary with Texaco.

Preceding pages: The wedding of members Leila Thompson and Kenneth Taratus took place in the First Church sanctuary on January 19, 1957.

Left: Dr. Fifield greets a young child, 1964.

Ruth and Naomi's volunteerism is not random; they work four days a week, all day, every week. "It is absolutely the most rewarding thing you can do," Ruth said.

But the sisters are not always serious. In fact, they are masters of back-to-back one-liners. "[Working] keeps us out of the malls," Naomi asserts. "Occasionally," Ruth adds, "someone asks, 'Are you still here?'"

Harry Fifield, the second pastor for whom Naomi worked, remembers her as "a truly superb secretary" and a "warm personal friend." He also remembers the one-liners. "One day," he wrote in *This Is the Church Being the Church* (published in 1993), "when I shouted gruffly, teasing her, 'Secretary, get in here,' there was dead silence. Suddenly she poked her head around the door and asked quietly, 'You growled, sir?'" Naomi remembers many things about Fifield, too, chief of which was his leadership through the difficult social upheavals of the 1950s, 1960s, and 1970s.

(Continues on page 68)

Music at First Church

usic is a gift from God," said Charles W. Whittaker, who currently serves as music director and organist at First Church. "It is a vibrant and expressive means of praise, meditation, and spiritual growth that speaks powerfully to us in ways words alone cannot."

Music has been an important part of worship at the church since its earliest days in frontier Atlanta, when founding pastor John Wilson played the melodeon in accompaniment to the singing of psalms. According to church legend, the singing of psalms gave way to hymns when they were introduced to the congregation by layman Carl O. Harmsen, appointed deacon in 1867. Like Dr. Wilson, Deacon Harmsen accompanied congregational singing on the melodeon, and he continued as music director until 1877, when Dr. Wilson's granddaughter, Julia Welborn, became organist. Mrs. Welborn held that position for twenty years.

In 1915, Dr. Wilson's great-grandson, Dr. Charles A. Sheldon Jr., became organist and held the position until 1952. People who sang in his choirs as children remember that he was quiet and retiring, and that he called them "chill'uns." In addition to his duties at First Church, Dr. Sheldon was organist at the Temple on Peachtree and the official city organist.

When Dr. Sheldon died in 1952, Mrs. Edith Howell Clark became organist and choir director and continued in that position until her retirement in 1964, an occasion, Dr. Fifield said, that brought tears to the eyes of his young son. "She was an excellent musician," Fifield observed,

"who continued the high standards of her much-loved predecessor." Mrs. Clark was the first director to institute the popular Christmas Eve candlelight service.

Longtime Minister of Music Charles Sheldon conducts a children's choir plus Dr. William V. Gardner in Winship Chapel.

Many of Atlanta's finest vocal soloists have been members of the First Church Chancel Choir, including this quartet of the 1970s: Sam Hagan, tenor (left); Jean Lemonds, soprano; Susan Poole, contralto; and Charles Horton, bass.

In 1964, the post of organist and music director was filled by Herbert S. Archer, an ordained minister, assisted by his wife, Mary Archer. The Archers presented both the finest of the classical sacred music and light contemporary works such as Buryl Red's gospel drama, *Celebrate Life,* which appealed to young people. During their twenty-five years as music directors, the Archers greatly strengthened the children and youth choir program. "Music was a way to teach them theology," Mary Archer said, "and provide a bonding experience." Besides staging biblical musicals complete with costumes, the Archers took the young people in their choirs on retreats and trips, one being a trip to the Holy Land, where the choirs sang in Bethlehem and Nazareth.

Some years before the Archers came to First Church, the Pilcher organ Dr. Sheldon designed had been replaced by a Moeller organ, but during their tenure it began showing signs of mechanical problems. "Sometimes in the middle of a service, a pipe would sound of its own volition," Reverend Archer said. "When that happened there was only way to stop the sound. A designated choir member left the choir loft and pulled out the offending pipe." In 1969, the Moeller was renovated and enlarged, and in 1992, the organ was further enhanced by extensive refurbishment and enlargement. The organ now boasts more than sixty-two hundred pipes played from a four-manual console in the choir loft. Also in 1992, a second, two-manual pipe organ was added in the church balcony. The new balcony console and the renovation and enlargement of the main organ were made possible through generous gifts from church families.

When Reverend and Mrs. Archer left in 1988, Charles and Diane Whittaker, both graduates of Westminster Choir College in Princeton, New Jersey, became co-organists, with Mr. Whittaker as director of music and Mrs. Whittaker as associate director. Today, they direct and oversee five

vocal choirs, a handbell choir (begun under the Archers), and a string ensemble made up of church members. They also developed the Musica Sacra Atlanta concert series, which presents outstanding artists as an outreach ministry. Like their predecessors, the Whittakers continue to offer fine sacred music, including both contemporary works and the great classical requiems, cantatas, and oratorios, each in its original language and accompanied by an orchestra. Under the Whittakers' direction, the First Church Chancel Choir was the principal choir at the church music festival in Salzburg, Austria, in 1990 and 1993. In 1990, the choir performed at the First Christmas of Freedom Festival in Czechoslovakia, and in 1995, they sang in England and Wales.

Atlanta was in the midst of a postwar boom when Harry Fifield arrived in 1953. Attracted by favorable business opportunities in a transportation hub and by the mild climate, thousands of new residents were coming to the city, many of whom were young men from the North who had received military training in the South; many others were "step-Southerners," people whose parents had grown up in the South and moved to the North seeking better opportunities. A *U.S. News and World Report* article published in the 1950s called the city "the main port of entry" into the New South. With the population surge, the suburbs and the city proper crept northward, and as a result, the gracious homes that once lined Peachtree Street around First Church began giving way to apartment buildings, boardinghouses, office buildings, service stations, and parking lots. In effect, the church that had left downtown now found itself in the city once again.

In the beginning of his ministry at First Church, Dr. Fifield was somewhat daunted by its sheer size. His Lynchburg church had seven hundred members; his new church numbered well over two thousand. In Lynchburg, his staff was made up of a pastor, secretary, director of Christian Education, combined organist–choir director, and janitor. Here the staff included the pastor and assistant pastor, a secretary for Christian Education,

hostess church secretary, business secretary, pastor's secretary, organist, and maintenance man, and almost as soon as Fifield arrived, officers of the church encouraged him to add more positions. Accordingly, in consultation with Assistant Pastor Allen Gardner, he compiled a wish list of new positions and, he said, "with tongue in cheek" gave it to the church officers, "sure it would be turned down." It wasn't.

During 1953, official of the Atlanta Presbytery asked that First Church help start a new congregation in the Sandy Springs area, and it complied by making a monetary contribution and advising its members living in the Sandy Springs area that a new church would soon be chartered. When Dr. Fifield presided over formation of Mount Vernon Presbyterian Church in May 1954, thirty of the ninety charter members had come from First Church.

When Allen Gardner left First Church during 1953 to pursue postgraduate studies at the University of Edinburgh, the church called William Ira Howell, pastor of the First Presbyterian Church of Hamlet, North Carolina, and he arrived in January 1954. Many church members recall Dr. Howell's inspiring Sunday-morning pastoral

First Church youths Dorothy Ragsdale and Betty King at Camp Smyrna.

prayers that seemed to flow effortlessly. They also remember his striking appearance. He had snow-white hair and a six-foot-five-inch-tall frame that earned him the nickname "Shorty." Dr. Fifield recalled that one Sunday when Howell was baptizing a four-year-old, the youngster said loudly, "Watch out, Shorty, that's cold!" Fifield recalled, but Howell wasn't fazed in the least as the congregation laughed. Howell served first as an assistant pastor, and then as an associate pastor, primarily in the area of pastoral care, until his retirement in 1972. "The congregation found him to be a deeply caring person," a church historian wrote, "always faithful and ready to help his people in time of need."

This aerial view shows First Church on Peachtree Street as it appeared in the 1950s.

Opposite: The Confirmation Class of 1958 is pictured in the Pioneer Department beneath the stained glass window Christ and the Children, given by Mrs. E. Bates Block in memory of her son, Robert Lowry Block.

In May 1954, a few months after Dr. Fifield came to First Church, events were set in motion that "would ultimately test and prove the caliber of First Presbyterian Church," he wrote. He was referring to the U.S. Supreme Court's decision in the *Brown v. the Board of Education of Topeka, Kansas,* case, striking down racial segregation in public schools. But neither First Church nor Fifield could have envisioned the next eighteen years,

Opposite: Dr. William Howell and a young parishioner, 1966. Dr. Fifield said that Dr. Howell reminded him of Shakespeare's description of Julius Caesar: "His life was gentle and the elements so mixed in him that nature might stand up and say to all the world, 'This was a man.'"

Below: This brochure of the early 1950s contains information on programs for all ages.

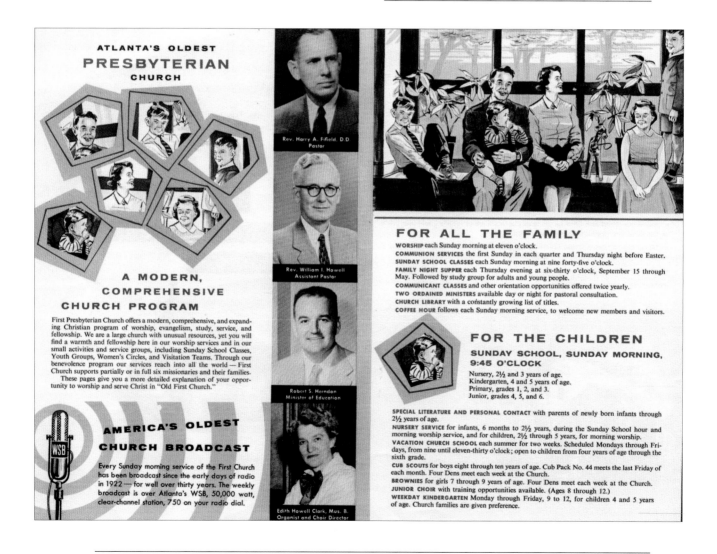

Dr. Harry Amos Fifield

At the end of the closing chapter of *This is the Church Being the Church*, written as a memoir after his retirement as senior pastor of First Church, Dr. Harry Amos Fifield chose to print a whimsical poem by church member Mai Belle Bradbury about the rigors of the ministry. It says in part:

With all of the problems that living imposes
A minister's life is no bed of roses.
Today a boost and tomorrow a knock
Trying to keep peace within your own flock,
Preaching of sin and its numerous terrors
Hoping you make no grammatical errors,
Watching the budget and stretching the dollar,
Christening the babies and hope they won't
*   holler . . .*
A few more months, Parson, so stay in
*   there pitching*
Then pick up your pole and say "Folks,
*   I've gone fishing."*

Dr. Fifield's inclusion of the poem attests to his own sense of humor, which helped carry him through the tumultuous years during which he served as pastor of First Church. Of those years he wrote, "I believe the Church's ministry in the mid-1900s was unique because of the peculiar challenges she faced and how she responded to the vigorous civil rights movement, the growing influx of international students, the hippie phenomenon, the stark tragedy of the Orly plane crash and other tests of the times. As she dealt forthrightly with these, I believe she was more and more the Church Christ wants her to be."

Dr. Fifield was born in Schenectady, New York, in 1910 and moved with his family to Florida in 1923. In 1933, he graduated from the University of Florida, where he had supported himself by playing drums in the college band and in an orchestra. He then entered Princeton Theological Seminary, and in 1936 received the Th.B. degree. He served as a chaplain in the U.S. Naval Reserve during World War II and was pastor of churches in Steelton, Pennsylvania; Deland, Florida; and Lynchburg, Virginia, before he and his wife, Margaret, came to First Church in 1953. After retiring in 1976, he served seventeen interim pastorates in South Carolina, Alabama, and Georgia. He has received honorary doctorates from Hampden Sydney College in Virginia and Oglethorpe University.

Of Dr. Fifield, church member and historian Nellie Jane Gaertner wrote, "His sermons never failed to move his hearers deeply, and frequently were ended with the challenge, 'And how is it with you?' He was unfailing as a loving pastor, ministering to the

needs of his people with deep concern and understanding. His wit was always ready for any challenge."

In his memoirs, Dr. Harry Fifield wrote, "I believe the Church's ministry in the mid-1900s was unique because of the peculiar challenges she faced and how she responded to the vigorous civil rights movement, the growing influx of international students, the hippie phenomenon, and the stark tragedy of the Orly plane crash. As she dealt forthrightly with these, I believe she was more and more the Church Christ wants her to be."

a period that would test the resolve of the congregation time and again.

Racial segregation was deeply rooted in the South, manifesting itself in every aspect of life. "[In Atlanta], absolutely everything was segregated," Rev. William Holmes Borders, pastor of the Wheat Street Baptist Church, told the authors of *Living Atlanta,* "the schools, the buses, the trains, the courthouse, the City Hall, the cemetery, . . . I passed through a period in Atlanta which might be rightfully labeled the dark days of bondage."

The entrenched racial segregation had not gone unnoticed by Presbyterians. The General Assembly of the national Presbyterian Church had wrestled with the problem for decades, Dr. Fifield said, "consistently declaring it to be wrong in the church." Addressing the issue again following the Supreme Court decision, the General Assembly sent letters to all congregations, asking them to take a Christian stand in the matter of race relations.

In the summer of 1954, the session of First Church cautiously complied with the request of the General Assembly by adopting the following resolution:

If Negroes should apply for membership in this Church, we suggest that they should meet with a committee to be elected by the Session who, together with the minister, will discuss the matter with them to endeavor to find their motives for requesting membership. The committee would then report to the Session and action on the application for membership would be taken by that body.

Three years later, the church's resolve in the matter of integration was directly tested. On Sunday, April 7, 1957, immediately following a sermon in which Dr. Fifield spoke against extremism on the part of either integrationists or segregationists, a member of the NAACP called his office and stated that a group of its members wanted to visit First Church the next Sunday. Elder Frank Holden told the caller she would be welcome, but should advise Dr. Fifield how many people would be coming so that space could be reserved. A meeting between the caller and Fifield was set for the following day.

Although the caller did not come to the scheduled meeting and her group did not come to church the next Sunday, action on the part of the church had been set in motion. On Monday night following the call, the session met to discuss how the matter could be dealt with. "Segregationists and integrationists entered the discussion

with vigor," Dr. Fifield wrote, "although I can recall no rancor." Some session members wanted to seat the visitors in the balcony or in the chapel, or insisted they be paraded to the front rows of the sanctuary. Some wanted to question their motives for coming before they were allowed to

This building on First Church grounds once served as the meeting place for Boy Scout Troop 60, which the church has sponsored since the 1920s. Troop 60 is the oldest continuously registered troop in Atlanta.

enter. But repeatedly in response to these suggestions, Fifield reported, Elder Hal Smith asked the question: "Gentlemen, is this what Jesus Christ would do?"

When the matter finally came to a vote, Fifield remembers, he said a prayer whose words he had not thought out, but which seemed to come to him. "Lord," he prayed, "once through your Servant you said, 'In Christ there is neither Jew nor Gentile, neither Greek nor barbarian, neither bond nor free, neither male nor female. . . .' Are you saying to us tonight, 'There is neither black nor white?'"

"That night," Fifield wrote, "the Session rose to its full stature." They voted to approve the following policy recommended by their Christian Action Committee, chaired by Elder Marthame Sanders Sr.:

If Negroes appear to attend the Worship or educational services of the Church, they are to be received and treated as any other Christians.

The reaction of many Georgia officials to the 1954 Supreme Court ruling calling for states to lay plans to end segregation in the public schools and the 1955 ruling calling for school segregation to be ended "with all deliberate speed" was to devise ways to prevent or at least postpone such action, even if it meant closing the public schools altogether. In 1957, feeling the need to clearly state the Judeo-Christian position on the matter, eighty Atlanta pastors, including Dr. Fifield, published a Ministers' Manifesto of six principles they believed Americans should uphold: freedom of speech, obedience to the law, preservation of the public schools, rejection of hatred and scorn for people because of their race or opinions, open communication between all responsible leaders, and recognition that difficulties cannot be solved through human strength or wisdom alone.

Prior to 1958, the violence that had begun to ignite in other Southern towns and cities in the wake of integration had left Atlanta untouched. As a result, wrote former police chief Herbert Jenkins in *Forty Years on the Force, 1932–1972*, "Atlanta, the city of shining Southern enlightenment . . . felt immune to . . . this kind of wanton destruction." That feeling of immunity ended on Sunday, October 12, 1958, when Atlantans awoke to the news that a predawn dynamite explosion had partially destroyed the unoccupied Temple of the Hebrew Benevolent Congregation, located on Peachtree Street. As soon as the 11 A.M. service at First Church was concluded that morning, the session met and voted to offer the Jewish congregation use of its

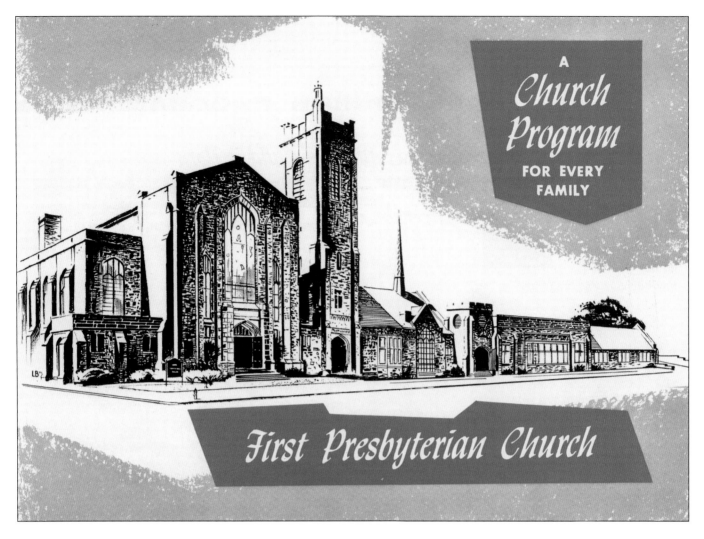

A
Church Program
FOR EVERY
FAMILY

First Presbyterian Church

facilities until their place of worship could be restored. The Temple accepted the offer and held meetings at First Church for the second time in its history, the first having occurred while the Jewish house of worship was being built in 1930.

The Temple bombing sent shock waves through the nation and roused Atlanta citizens to greater vigilance against further violence. In November following the October bombing, a second Ministers' Manifesto was issued, this time signed by

This 1958 brochure announces the building expansion program that would add a fellowship hall and more Sunday School rooms and enlarge Winship Chapel.

312 Atlanta ministers and rabbis. The second Manifesto upheld the first and appealed to churches and synagogues to promote free discussion of the issues of integration, and to community

and state leaders to find creative ways to keep the public schools open; requested appointment of a citizens' commission to preserve harmony; and called on citizens to solve the problems of racism "humbly, patiently, in a spirit of realism and with God's help."

In the wake of the Temple bombing, First Church's Christian Relations Committee went on record opposing the closing of the public schools, and the following spring the Christian Education Program initiated reciprocal visits with other churches and religious groups.

As the 1950s drew to a close, the church could look back on several expanded programs and new initiatives undertaken during the decade. Among them were a duplicate Sunday worship service (at 8:45) begun in 1950 to accommodate the increasing membership; a church library established in 1952 under sponsorship of the Berean and Women's Bible classes; weekly Family Night Suppers begun in 1954; and begun in 1956, an Annual Dinner and

Former mayor Ivan Allen and First Church pastor Dr. George Wirth. Besides Allen, two other First Church members once briefly served as Atlanta mayors: Elder William Markham (1853) and John Glen (1855).

Congregational Meeting, and a Coffee Hour following each 11 o'clock service.

On Sunday, August 7 1960, the "kneel-ins" occurring all over the South came to First Church, when, midway through the worship service, eight members of the Student Nonviolent Coordinating Committee walked into the sanctuary and seated themselves among the congregation. After the service, which proceeded without incident, one student left a note bearing a powerful message. It said, in part:

As believers in the fatherhood of God and the brotherhood of man, we humbly seek to worship with you in fulfillment of Christ's commandment that His children may be one in Him even as He is one in God.

Perhaps chief among Atlanta's leaders calling for peaceful compliance with the school desegregation order were two visionary mayors, William Berry Hartsfield and his successor, Ivan Allen Jr., a First Church deacon. Convinced that closing the public schools would spell disaster, Hartsfield said in 1960, "It will do little good to bring about more architecture and concrete while a shocked and amazed world looks at a hundred thousand innocent children roaming the streets." By 1961, the last year of his twenty-five-year

MESSIAH

A SACRED ORATORIO

For many years, First Church choirs have performed the finest liturgical music.

mayor to do so. Initially his support of integration had arisen out of the pragmatic belief that it would be good for business, but gradually his motivation changed. "As I became more involved, I found that conditions [in the lives of black people] were more difficult than I had thought," he said. "I finally crossed over and made my commitment on a purely personal basis."

In 1962, tragedy unrelated to the civil rights movement suddenly struck the city and First Church. Early in May, a group of 106 art patrons, including 12 First Church members, flew to Europe to visit galleries under the sponsorship of the Atlanta Art Association. On Sunday morning, June 3, the group boarded a Boeing 707 at Orly Airport in Paris for the trip back home. As the plane raced down the runway, trouble developed. The aircraft ran off the end of the runway and slammed into a stone cottage. Everyone on board died except three flight attendants seated in the tail section that in the collision broke free of the plane.

Word reached Dr. Fifield as soon as he concluded the early worship service. Naomi Byrd remembers that during the Sunday School hour, children whose parents had been killed were taken out of classes, and it became Fifield's duty to tell them about the tragedy that would change their lives. Meanwhile, Dr. Howell

administration, Hartsfield had shepherded steps to integrate the city's golf courses, public transportation, libraries, police force, and schools.

Shortly after his 1961 election, Allen testified before Congress in favor of passage of the Civil Rights Bill, the only Southern

and Youth Director Bill Boyce set out for the homes of bereaved families. Pastor of Administration and Education Fred Widmer conducted the opening part of the 11 A.M. worship service, while in his study Fifield changed the sermon he had planned to deliver, centering his revised remarks on the Cross and the Resurrection.

Mayor Allen, who flew to Paris to represent the victims' families, wrote in his book, *Mayor: Notes on the Sixties:* "It was difficult to describe the feeling I had as we looked through the charred wreckage. . . . There was no precedent for this kind of agony." *Atlanta Constitution* Editor Eugene Patterson wrote: "These were the caring men and the gentle women who . . . lifted our eyes to the things that matter, to the meanings that history remembers when it has discarded the pettiness of wars and riches and little movements—to the arts, the culture that endures. These people were irreplaceable."

In 1968, the newly constructed Memorial Arts Center (now the Woodruff Arts Center), situated across Sixteenth Street from First Church and housing the Atlanta Symphony, Atlanta College of Art, Alliance Theater, and High Museum of Art, was dedicated to the memory of the art patrons who lost their lives at Orly Airport.

On the night of April 4, 1968, word of another tragedy reached Atlanta. Civil rights leader Martin Luther King Jr., an Atlantan, had been shot outside a motel in Memphis, Tennessee. Soon after Mayor Allen and his wife, Louse Richardson Allen, saw the bulletin on a television screen in their home, they drove to Dr. King's home and escorted his wife, Coretta Scott King, to the airport, where she was to board a plane for Memphis. "They had been at the airport only a moment when the news came," Harold Martin wrote in volume three of *Atlanta and Environs.* "Dr. King was dead. There was no need now to rush to Memphis, so they went back to the King house, in silence, shocked and dazed."

As the evening wore on, Mayor Allen received a call from legendary Co-ca-Cola leader, philanthropist, and First Church member Robert W. Woodruff. In *Mayor,* Allen recalls Woodruff's words:

> *"Ivan," he said, "the minute they bring King's body back tomorrow between then and the time of the funeral Atlanta, Georgia, is going to be the center of the universe." He paused. "I want you to do whatever is right and necessary, and whatever the city can't pay for will be taken care of. Just do it right."*

As Allen and his staff began to realize that the city soon would have to provide accommodations for the hundreds of thousands of people sure to pour into Atlanta for the funeral, word began to filter in that churches and individuals in the city were opening their doors to the visitors. One of those was First Church. Members made thousands of sandwiches for visitors all over the city, and the night before the funeral the church housed many visitors on its second and third floors. As the visitors left the church on the morning of the funeral, Fifield wrote, "one after another expressed their surprise that a white church would open its doors and its heart [to them]." Behind the mule-drawn wagon bearing the body of Dr. Martin Luther King Jr. to Ebenezer Baptist Church that day streamed a crowd of nearly two hundred thousand.

∼∽

On May 18, 1969, First Church's experience with the civil rights movement reached a climax, Fifield wrote, "when three black men suddenly appeared, interrupted our worship service and stretched the nerves of both ministers and congregation." Representatives of the National Black Economic Development Conference, based in Detroit, made their way to a place close to the pulpit and read the Black Militants' Manifesto. The Manifesto, which was being read nationwide, demanded reparations totaling $500 million from churches and synagogues for wrongs committed against black people over the centuries. First Church's portion of the reparations, the men read, would amount to one-sixth of its yearly income.

As the men entered and read the Manifesto, Dr. Fifield spoke quietly to them, and when they left quietly as he had asked, he pronounced the benediction. Members marveled at his seeming unflappability. "He was just so calm and nice," Naomi Byrd remembers telling Dr. Howell. "You weren't sitting behind him," Howell replied. "His knees were shaking."

When the militants returned the following Sunday, Mayor Allen was sitting in a parked car outside the church, ready to step in if there was trouble, but this time the men were prevented from entering the sanctuary, and they agreed to come to a 6 P.M. meeting. At the meeting, Dr. Fifield read a statement saying that the church already spent thousands of dollars each year ministering to blacks and whites and others at home and abroad and would not accede to the

Sisters Naomi Byrd and Ruth Law have been faithful First Church members some fifty years.

During the 1960s and 1970s, the alternative hippie culture flourished in the Tenth Street area of midtown.

militants' demands. The men expressed disappointment, but they left quietly and made no further demands.

Four years after the militants visited First Church, a young black man from Cameroon who had heard WSB broadcasts of the worship service presented himself for membership. Lewis M. Ngalame, in Atlanta preparing for Christian service in Africa, was unanimously received by the session, becoming the first black member since the days of slavery.

Occurring in part simultaneously with the civil rights movement was the hippie movement of the 1960s and 1970s. In Atlanta, the youths Harold Martin described as "long-haired young men and their long-skirted, barefooted girlfriends" began to concentrate around the boarding house community in the Tenth Street area, almost on the doorstep of First Church. "Some came from alcoholic parents and broken homes," Dr. Fifield said. "Some were simply rebelling against . . . contemporary society. Some girls turned to prostitution in order to live. Drug abuse was widespread."

What was the church's role, if any, in relation to these neighbors? Since no concerted neighborhood ministry had been undertaken before, there was no precedent on which to act. "[The church's] doors were open to anyone,"

Fifield recorded in his memoirs. "She had expanded her facilities [to take care of her own]. She had a well-known radio ministry and contributed substantially both to world and to national missions. But [this kind of] ministry to the neighborhood about her just [had not been] her concern."

One of the first people in the church to become involved with the

Rev. Robert W. Bevis, who came to First Church in 1969, was a guiding force in the formation of the Ecumenical Community Ministry.

hippies was Youth Pastor Alex Williams, a native of Walton County, Georgia, with degrees from Emory University and Columbia Theological Seminary, whom

Fifield called "a brilliant theologian with a strong sense of social consciousness." "The truth is," Williams said, "that as far as I was concerned, First Presbyterian Church was on trial. I wondered if she would make a go of a Christian ministry to these young people. . . ." Through Williams's influence, Dr. Frank Walker, then chairman of the church deacons and president of the Fulton County Medical Society, established a medical clinic for the young people in the church's Scout Hut on the church property.

Shortly after the clinic was established, Williams began pressing for a Christian Center and persuaded several members to go with him to a crude social center the hippies had set up in an abandoned house in the Tenth Street area. The scene was appalling. "It was about 11 P.M," Elder A.B. Padgett remembers. "We visited this place where young people had passed out on benches and on tables. Some among us who had opposed any church involvement with the hippies were stunned. They had not really been cognizant of what was going on. As a result, we had to consider our challenge to 'Do unto others as you would have them do unto you.'"

First Church became the primary sponsor of a center on Tenth street called Atlanta Aurora, which opened July 1, 1970. The center offered counseling, Bible study, a drug abuse program, adult education, and worship services, and made showers, washing machines, and sewing machines available. In addition to this work with Aurora, Williams briefly conducted a Sunday School class called "Ministering to the Hippie Community," attended in part by the hippies themselves. Dr. Fifield vividly remembers the sight of "long-haired, barefoot youth in ragged blue jeans heading for the classroom and then to the worship service" of the old, tradition-steeped church, and after the service, shaking his hand and thanking "First Presbyterian Church for caring."

By the time Williams left First Church in 1972 to serve as Presbyterian pastor to the campus of the University of Georgia, the hippie culture was fading as many of the youths simply returned home, and by the mid-1970s a revitalization of the Tenth Street area was under way.

As the mission of the church had begun fully to embrace its community, more and more members expressed their faith by serving others. In 1971, the outreach ministry was made an official part of the agenda when A.B. Padgett was appointed chairman of a new coordinating body called the Community Witness and Service Committee, and in 1973, Rev. Robert W. Bevis, who had come to First Church in 1969 as pastor of education, was named the first associate pastor for Community

Ministry. At his installation to this new post, Elder Alice Brown said, "We see you . . . as one who keeps us . . . grounded in the theological basis for involvement in the world. . . . Bob, you have a responsibility to make us uncomfortable." In the years to come, Reverend Bevis would continue and expand on many fronts the work Alex Williams had begun.

To Harry Fifield, the church's evolving concept of its mission during the mid-1900s was no accident. "[Christ] walks along Peachtree," he had said in a 1970 sermon. "God has gotten right down into our experience—with us who live and love and cry and die along Peachtree Street. . . . He is still changing lives there, forgiving sins, molding character, answering prayers. His presence with you and me depends on the hospitality of our hearts."

Harry Fifield retired in 1976 after serving with distinction through twenty-three challenging years, crucial in the history of Atlanta and First Church. He was succeeded by Dr. Robert Eugene Randolph, who came from his pastorate at the Presbyterian church in Signal Mountain, Tennessee, and served as interim pastor until 1977. That year, First Church called Rev. Paul Thornton Eckel, then a doctoral candidate at San Francisco Theological Seminary, who had served churches in New Jersey, Maryland, Virginia, and South Carolina.

Chapter V

The Church at the Dawn of a New Millennium

"Therefore, since we are surrounded by so great a cloud of witnesses, let us also lay aside every weight, and sin which clings so closely, and let us run with perseverance the race that is set before us, looking to Jesus, the pioneer and perfecter of our faith, . . ."

Hebrews 12:1–2

Each week some fifty volunteers work to prepare and serve the Sunday Morning Homeless Prayer Breakfast.

Just after daybreak on a Sunday morning in October 1996, the first frost of autumn glistens on the grass as hundreds of men and women walk toward the stone church at the corner of Peachtree and Sixteenth. These people who have come from all over the city are part of the homeless population. Arriving hunched against an unseasonably brisk chill, they enter the warmth of Fifield Hall. A corps of volunteers serves juice and hot coffee, while others prepare vats of grits and mounds of toast, ham, boiled eggs, doughnuts, and fruit.

One of the volunteers this morning is Winfred Jones. Once homeless himself, Jones knows the life well. He remembers walking and walking and always looking down. He remembers trying to maintain some pride by changing once a week into "Sunday clothes" he hid behind a bush in a city park. He remembers that people smiled at him in the soup kitchens.

He remembers the fear: "Homeless people are afraid all the time," he says.

Jones is one of the fortunate ones who find their way out after a long struggle. Trying to escape his fear and his drug addiction, he says, he began to pray. "I knew that perfect love casts out fear. I started to thank God all during the day. As I walked, I was always finding a lot of pennies. Every time I found one, I would say, 'Praise the Lord.' One day I came to First Church, and I said to [Rev. Charles Black], 'I think I'm ready to quit.'"

While the homeless people eat their meal this morning, Associate Pastor for Community Ministries Charles Black, about whom Jones speaks, talks to them and prays with them. As those who have finished their meal leave with bags of fruit, some stop by a volunteer seated in the hall. She is conducting a referral service, telling them how to get medical and other kinds of help, and giving out tickets for the showers and clean clothes available on Sunday nights at the church.

When all the people have eaten, the kitchen volunteers and some of the homeless guests clean the tables. In the now nearly empty room, one homeless man goes to the piano and plays Beethoven's "Fur Elise."

The Breakfast for the Homeless had its origin in 1981 when an informal worship service and continental breakfast for members was held at 8:45 A.M. each Sunday in Fifield Hall. "A few homeless people, four or five, began to come," said elder Mary Joe Dellinger, who has been a volunteer leader in the homeless ministry since its inception, and is currently its chairperson. "Suddenly, one Sunday, the number increased. They just poured in. We moved the worship service back to the sanctuary and did only the breakfast in the fellowship hall." By 1983, between 100 and 150 homeless people were being fed each Sunday, and today the average number has climbed to more than 500.

The Women's Shelter, begun in the winter of 1981–82, grew out of the Sunday breakfasts when Dr. Eckel discovered that a woman who had been attending had no home and was living in a cardboard lean-to behind Piedmont Hospital. "I asked her innocently, 'Where do you live?'" Dr. Eckel remembers. "And she said, 'Do you really want to know?' I found what she told me utterly intolerable. I asked the session to help, and they came back almost immediately with the decision to go ahead with plans to house this woman and others." For five months that winter, sleeping space for these women was set aside in the church on an ad hoc basis. During the summer of 1982, the shelter closed temporarily while a wing of

Every evening all year long, twelve women find warmth, care, hot food, clean clothes, a comfortable bed, and a certain security at the Women's Shelter.

the third floor was renovated to provide permanent quarters for twelve women at a time. Since reopening in November 1982, the shelter has provided an evening meal, a place to sleep, and shower and laundry facilities for hundreds of women.

Each month, some eighty volunteers spend a night or bring food for the shelter. Volunteers also help stabilize the women's lives by assisting them in finding jobs and places to live before they move out of the protected environment. A woman who left the shelter and now is living independently wrote:

The main thing you notice about the shelter is how many different kinds of people there are here. . . . Some have been street people for a long time. Some have mental health problems. Others were holding their own in the world until they met with a crisis or series of crises. In most cases it took an accumulation of events before we were not able to provide for ourselves. . . . At a time when I felt unwanted or unwelcome anywhere else, [there were] relationships and relating going on. . . . After you lose your job and lose your apartment, you do a simple thing like wiping the table after supper. . . . It makes you feel good.

When the Sunday Morning Prayer Breakfast for the Homeless and the Women's Shelter were begun in

1981 and 1982, they were the latest of many new community ministries. A concerted distribution of food had been initiated in 1971, when the church began to deliver U.S. Department of Agriculture surplus food to families in the Techwood Homes area. In 1978, this effort continued under the Meals-On-Wheels program. During the first year of Meals-On-Wheels, twelve meals were delivered three times each week. Today, the ministry, chaired by Julie Wyant, involves seventy-five volunteers delivering an average of eighty-five meals every day to homebound people.

The Venable Food Pantry, another effort to feed needy people, was established during Dr. Fifield's ministry by the late Mary Elizabeth Venable, first chairperson of the church's Hunger Issues Committee. In 1995, the Pantry, partially sponsored by the Women's Bible Class, distributed twenty-seven hundred bags of food to hungry people who came to First Church and to other emergency services.

In 1962, church members Frances Elyea and Caroline Bethea, who also were teachers at Spring Street School, began to tutor at-risk students newly enrolled in that school in space provided at First Church. The after-school program was so successful it was expanded to include a summer session offering Bible study, crafts, games, and field trips. Continuing the teaching ministry, First Church offered its facilities for use in training illiterate people in the early 1970s. Also in the seventies, Reverend Bevis and members of the Women of the Church ministered to women prisoners at the Fulton County jail through classes in Bible study, sewing, and crafts. Around 1984, the church began offering conversational English classes for members of the international community.

In 1980, the church received the Community Service Award of the Mental Health Association of Metropolitan Atlanta for its work with de-institutionalized mental patients living in nearby boardinghouses. Begun in 1979, the Boarding House Ministry offered a hot supper, worship, and fellowship on Sunday evenings. Also aiding mental patients was a Wednesday morning art therapy class and hot lunch begun in 1980. Today, the Alice Brown Art Therapy Ministry, named for the church member chiefly responsible for its establishment, carries out its work in cooperation with Grady Hospital. In the early 1980s, the church set up an emergency Clothes Closet to distribute donations, and in recent years, the Clothes Closet ministry has expanded to allow needy people to shower and wash their clothes.

In 1991, under the ministry of Dr. Jerry Wright, then associate pastor for

Care Ministries, the church began a new ministry for senior adults called Come On Along, and a ministry to disabled people called the Accessibility Ministry for Full Membership (AM/FM), which has taken a leadership role in metropolitan-wide efforts to break down both physical and psychological barriers to church worship. Also in 1991, through a gift in memory of business leader and church member Frank Carter, the church initiated the Business and Professional Luncheon Ministry, featuring quarterly speakers who focus on workday issues from a Christian perspective.

When Dr. Fifield arrived at First Church in 1953, he found that some twenty international students from local colleges were affiliate members, and in succeeding years he watched the number increase. In 1970, when the Atlanta Christmas International House was initiated, First Church set up cots in Sunday School rooms and housed many students unable to return to their homelands for the holidays. This program continues today, with students housed in the homes of members.

In 1975, the church strengthened its international ministry by forming a Sunday School class for international people in Atlanta. The class has chiefly been guided since its inception by Rev. Fahed Abu-Akel, who as a young Palestinian Christian from Israel had begun working with the youth and elderly of the church when he was a student at Columbia Theological Seminary. Today, the class continues to provide an introductory look at Christianity for many, and for all, a comfortable atmosphere in which to share their experiences and receive support as they cope with life in a foreign country. Expressing his thanks for the church's hospitality, student Kayode Dada wrote:

> . . . [The foreign student who comes to Atlanta] is struggling to understand the new method of instruction . . . to cope with the southern accent . . . to know the shopping malls . . . to keep his faith intact. He is totally confused. Then the good Samaritans of First Presbyterian Church of Atlanta quietly come into his life. The International Sunday School class invites him to their meeting. For the first time since he has been here, he meets someone who can speak his native tongue. . . . He begins to appreciate the earth as a small world.

Also in 1975, the international ministry began helping to relocate Vietnamese refugees coming to this country, and this ministry continues today, also embracing refugees from

Dr. Paul T. Eckel

Or. Paul Thornton Eckel was born in Kobe, Japan, to an American family who were teachers and missionaries there before World War II. Much of his youth was spent in Florida and Washington, D.C., and he went on to earn the divinity degree from Princeton Theological Seminary and the Doctor of Ministry degree from San Francisco Theological Seminary.

Dr. Eckel's pastoral ministry has been with churches in Virginia, suburban Washington, D.C., South Carolina, Georgia, and Kansas. He served as senior pastor at First Church from 1977 to 1988, a time when the congregation was still adapting to the sweeping social changes that began in the 1960s. Under Dr. Eckel's leadership, the church employed its first woman and African American pastors and continued to enlarge its community ministry. He points with particular pride to establishment of the Women's Shelter, which, he said, "has ministered to hundreds of women" and has been carried out entirely by volunteers, including Mary Joe Dellinger, "who has made it her life's work."

Accompanied by his wife, Jan, Dr. Eckel has, since 1988, been engaged in a national preaching and teaching ministry overseen by the Florida-based Renewal Ministries Foundation, which he serves as president.

101

Since 1990, First Church has offered help and encouragement to Vietnamese refugees An and Thuy Do and their family. An (above) is a skilled woodworker.

an ecumenical ministry of hospitality and friendship directed since its inception by Dr. Abu-Akel out of offices at First Church. Under Abu-Akel's leadership, this ministry to thousands of students each year has become a model for other cities to emulate. Today, members of the AMIS board of directors and standing committees come from First Church, Ebenezer Baptist Church, Northside United Methodist Church, Oglethorpe Presbyterian Church, St. James United Methodist Church, St. Martin in the Fields Episcopal Church, and the Presbytery of Greater Atlanta.

Other efforts in the international ministry include support of foreign missions; Villa International, a hospitality center for foreign physicians and researchers studying in the city; scholarships for international students studying in Atlanta; and partnerships with fellow Christians in Haiti, Kenya, and Brazil.

During his years as community minister, Reverend Bevis was the guiding force behind the ever-enlarging program. In 1975, he helped initiate talks that led to a far-reaching

other nations. In 1976, the church helped establish the Atlanta Ministry with International Students (AMIS),

effort called the Ecumenical Community Ministry (ECM), involving four churches: First Presbyterian, Trinity Presbyterian, Cascade United Methodist, and St. Bartholomew's Episcopal. By self-definition, ECM was "a contemporary model of the church's faithfulness to the clear, direct biblical mandate to care for the poor, oppressed and afflicted of our time."

In 1975, as Reverend Bevis prepared to undertake the organization's work as community pastor for all four churches, he said in a sermon, "What comes charging out of the past is the call to be love-in-action. Jesus was and is love-in-action. . . . We dare not confine God to approved channels. God is not that small. . . . The heart of the Gospel is not a rule of safety, but an adventure of the spirit."

In 1976, ECM began an apartment ministry of support and service at Carver Homes, the city's second largest public housing project, and helped initiate AMIS. The same year the ministry to Carver Homes was begun, it was enlarged to include Carver High School, principally due to the collaborative efforts of A.B. Padgett and Dr. Norris Hogans, then the newly appointed principal of the high school and now a First Church elder.

Dr. Hogans had found urgent need at Carver. "The average income of the families was five thousand dollars a year per family, and the average family had seven members," he said. "Students who were discipline problems and girls who got pregnant in other high schools were sent to Carver High School. At one time, there were eighty-five pregnant girls there. There was a laundry list of needs. There was poverty and despair.

"A.B. and I had worked together on other community projects, and we had formed a partnership," Hogans said. "We called ourselves salt and pepper. He was the salt, I was the pepper. He was the white guy, I was the black guy."

In the Carver community, ECM set up a health center and day care center, carried out job training and placement, provided adult education and enrichment programs, and led activities for children, among other things. The First Church volunteer Hogans remembers best is Alice Brown. "She would come every day and work until nine or ten at night," he said. "She was amazing. She had so much patience. This is what impressed me so with the church. The people who came to help had tenacity and endurance and tolerance. These people were for real."

Today, First Church continues its involvement in the Carver ministry,

Dr. George Bryant Wirth

Among the artifacts in George Bryant Wirth's conference room is a set of small bronze cursive letters that seem to race downhill. SLOW DOWN, the letters spell. This may be a message to himself, but by all accounts he seldom heeds it. "He is always in motion," said Naomi Byrd, who has served First Church as secretary to seven pastors. "I would have given a million dollars to have been younger and worked with George, but I realized I could never keep up with him."

"George has ideas and he is willing to work for them," Elder Hal Smith said. "His relationships with people have made the church come alive. George is a fireball."

Dr. Wirth grew up in the historic old whaling town of Sag Harbor, Long Island, the oldest of the four children of Presbyterian Pastor George Robert Wirth. At age fourteen, he entered Stony Brook Preparatory School in Stony Brook, New York. After graduation, he enrolled at the University of North Carolina at Chapel Hill, where he earned a degree in journalism in 1969. He received the master of divinity degree from Princeton Theological Seminary in 1972 and the doctor of ministry degree from Pittsburgh Theological Seminary in 1990, and served churches in Bryn Mawr and Sewickley, Pennsylvania, before coming to the First Presbyterian Church of Atlanta in 1990. His many activities have included service as a trustee of Davis & Elkins College in Elkins, West Virginia; Stony Brook School; Princeton Seminary; Warren Wilson College in Swannanoa, North Carolina; The Westminster Schools in Atlanta; the Carter Center; and the Woodruff Arts Center in Atlanta. He and his wife, Barbara Morrison Wirth, have two children, Alyson and Matthew.

Until late in his senior year at UNC, George Wirth planned to build a career in communications, perhaps in the field of advertising. "I was focused on making my mark," he said. "I would even describe myself as driven toward that." One March day that year, he walked by the University Presbyterian Church in Chapel Hill and heard singing coming

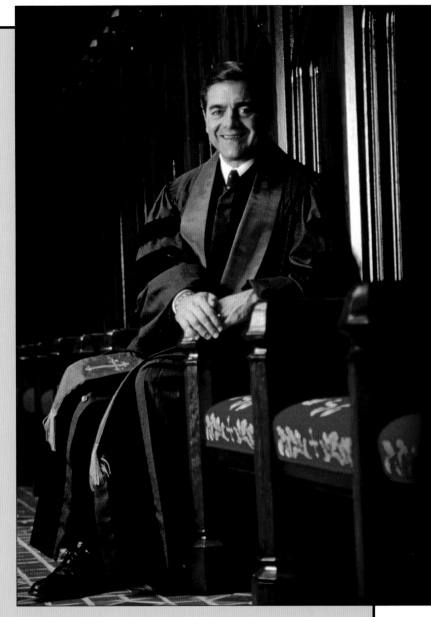

from inside. He wandered into the church, where a missionary to Brazil was speaking. "He quoted T.S. Eliot's 'The Hollow Men,'" Dr. Wirth remembers. "It contains the words: 'These are the hollow men.' I realized that message was being directed to me. I had been able to get pretty far on my own stamina, ability, skill, and yet inside me there was an emptiness, a void. I prayed in that church that God would help me fill up what was hollow. Within one week of that experience, I decided to enroll in the seminary.

"I believe everyone has something in them that is good and also something that is hollow. I see that as part of my ministry: to be part of the process of bringing the spirit of Christ, which has the filling capacity, into people's lives."

Somewhere near the SLOW DOWN sign in Dr. Wirth's conference room is another that reads: "Blessed are those who inspire the people through word and deed, for they shall be called ministers," and still another that in small wooden letters reads simply "Jesus."

supporting summer camp attendance, field trips, honors and athletic banquets, and SAT preparation for children and youth; the Carver Granny House for children whose parents are in drug treatment; and the Friends of Carver and Share Project support networks, among other efforts.

In the summer of 1981, as Atlanta discovered that a growing number of black children and youth were either missing or had been murdered, Reverend Bevis was given a leave of absence to head a task force to deal with the resulting unrest. Under his leadership, a citywide program called Help the Children offered activities for youth modeled after the Carver program. In 1982, Bevis received the Community Service Award of the Christian Council of Metropolitan Atlanta, and the First Church session received the Ecumenical Service Award of the General Assembly of the Presbyterian Church for its work through ECM.

In 1985, Reverend Bevis announced his intention to leave First Church because of poor health, and a search committee set out to find a new community minister. In 1988, the church called Rev. Charles Black, then residing in Atlanta and serving as a member of the staff of the Mission Board of the Presbyterian Church.

Reverend Black had heard about the position through Betty Sanders, a First Church member who served on the Mission Board staff with him. "She said, 'Hey, would you be interested in this position?'" Black remembers. He didn't think she was serious. Charles Black did not believe that First Church would be hiring an African American pastor.

But Sanders was serious. She brought him information about the position and encouraged him to update his résumé. "I have told them about you," she said. "I think they are very interested in you." Black began to talk with the search committee in the fall of 1987 and the church called him in January 1988.

Taking up his new position, Black found that Bob Bevis had left in place a strong ministry carried out by a faithful core group of volunteer lay people. "Those were and are the people carrying the load of the ministry, in a very gracious kind of way," he said. "I as a pastor relate to them and try to provide the environment they need to do the ministries, but many hands participate in the work."

Still, Reverend Black was not immediately accepted by some in the church who regarded him as minister to the community but not their minister. That began to change as

Black, trained as a hospital chaplain, visited members who were ill. "As I began to take Communion to people in the hospitals and to people's homes," he said, "gradually the way they saw me evolved. At first I would often be introduced as 'the pastor for outreach.' Then, in a year or so, people would say, 'He is one of our pastors.' I had known [my entry into the life of the church] would take time. I had known that this would not be just a job. But somehow or another I was called by God and this congregation to do ministry here in this place."

To Eleanor Dabney, the explanation for the acceptance of Reverend Black at First Church is simple. "He loved us into accepting him," she said.

Besides the many official aspects of this work, Black ministers to the ten to fifteen people who walk to the church and some twenty more who call every day asking for some kind of help.

Elder Norris Hogans, Elder A.B. Padgett, and Rev. Charles Black have long been leaders in First Church's Community Ministry.

"Many of those who come here have been walking a long time," he said. "They need showers, clean clothes, food, MARTA tokens. I usually meet them downstairs. Before I go to them, I tell myself, 'You are about to meet a person who is the Body of Christ.' The person waiting is Christ himself. If we forget that, we may forget to really be with them. To love them. But also to ask the tough questions.

"When they come they look tired and haggard. But when they leave, they have been refreshed. They go back out the door and try it again.

"Sometimes they come not because they need something, but just to say, 'Thank you.' Often this happens when I have begun to be discouraged. Those are the times when I realize again that the ministry works two ways. We who minister begin to identify our own brokenness as we look at the brokenness of others.

"We are all on a journey. One beggar asks another beggar for bread. We are all pilgrim people, called out, not in. Called out into the world."

In 1996, Reverend Black accepted the Community Service Award, again given to First Church by the Christian Council of Metropolitan Atlanta.

In 1977, when Dr. Paul Eckel was considering the search committee's call to become senior pastor of First Church, he remembers asking committee members, "What in the world do [you] expect me to do with this great thing here on this corner, this big building and all of its people? Everything seems to be going fine.' They said, 'We want two things: First, some spiritual leadership, and second, someone who will preach the word faithfully from the pulpit.'"

Accepting the call, he joined a church with four associate pastors, a support staff of twenty-one employees, and three lay professional staff persons. Also in the building were four affiliate community ministry organizations, each with its own staff. During his years as senior pastor, Dr. Eckel saw growth in both the church's community ministry and its member-to-member ministry, particularly through Care Fellowship and the Stephen Ministry. Preparing lay people to teach, Dr. Eckel, a superb preacher and inspiring teacher himself, began in 1980 to lead the first two-year session of the Bethel Bible Series, designed to provide a knowledgeable overview of both the Old and New Testaments.

In 1985, sensing "that First Church needed to move in the direction of a television ministry," Dr. Eckel introduced the idea to the session, which quickly approved it. Accordingly,

Reverend Charles Black leads the Prayer of Confession at First Church's Rededication Service in 1996.

regular Sunday services were videotaped and edited to produce half-hour services for a television audience, programming that continues to expand today. For several years, Dr. Eckel and Reverend Abu-Akel co-led groups of church members on pilgrimages to the Holy Land, and they led one trip to Greece to trace the footsteps of the Apostle Paul. Dr. Eckel also served as chairperson for the Atlanta Presbytery's PATH (Presbyterian Answer to Hunger) program, which his wife, Jan Eckel, administered for five years.

During Dr. Eckel's ministry, First Church in 1985 called Rev. Mary Lynn Tobin as associate pastor for Church Growth and Rev. Charles Black in 1988 as associate pastor for Community Ministries, thus making them the first ordained woman and African American to serve on the staff.

In the annual report published in 1988, the last year of Dr. Eckel's ministry at First Church, he called attention to the church's purchase of a new bus, repairs of facilities, landscaping and new signage on Peachtree Street, and plans to provide handicapped access to the buildings. "Here at Peachtree and Sixteenth," he concluded, "we continue to marvel at the vigorous expansion going on within the Midtown area. Ours is certainly one of the most dynamic areas of development in Atlanta. Opportunities for spiritual growth, congregational expansion, and mission challenge are enormous. As we enter the last years of the 1980s and prepare for the final decade of this century, let us do so with optimism, enthusiasm, and conviction that there is much to accomplish together as we follow our Lord faithfully."

As Dr. Eckel left First Church in 1988 to become a full-time evangelist, replacing him was Dr. J. Davison Philips, who came out of retirement from Columbia Theological Seminary, where he had served as president, to once again work with First Church, this time as an interim pastor (he was an assistant pastor at First Church from 1947 to 1950). Dr. Philips's strong and skillful administration and pastoral care helped the congregation through its time of transition and endeared him to everyone as a spiritual leader and friend. By 1990, the search committee looking for a senior pastor had recommended Dr. George Bryant Wirth, from the Sewickley Presbyterian Church in suburban Pittsburgh.

"I was called here by a committee who started coming to Sewickley in September 1989," Dr. Wirth remembers. "After their first visit, I wrote Dr. [William L.] Pressly, a member of the committee, and said I did not believe they should pursue calling me. I was happy where I was. He wrote me a letter, which I saved and treasure. He said:

I take this liberty on the basis of my being eighty-one and twice your age. As a headmaster [of The Westminster Schools in Atlanta] who has advised and counseled hundreds of students and teachers, . . . I feel sincerely that you have made your decision not to come before you gathered all the facts. . . . This letter is sent to you prayerfully. I . . . ask that you and Barbara pray long and hard before you answer it. May God lead you to give us a chance.

"That letter got us on the plane to Atlanta," Dr. Wirth said. "In January of 1990, the church voted to call me as their pastor. I now believe I was called here through those people and the voice of the Spirit of God. That is very important to me."

Dr. Wirth remembers that as he approached Atlanta for the first time by car, he thought, *This city is shining. This is a shining city on a hill!*

"I saw the skyscrapers," he said, "but I was looking for the steeples. I

Eleven volunteers work throughout the year to televise First Church's Sunday morning services, which reach some 60,000 viewers.

knew the city was full of steeples, and I was looking for them. The tall steepled churches have been called by Christ to touch the lives of the people who work in the skyscrapers.

"I am grateful that this church is at the center of the metropolis called Atlanta. There is a diversity here that God has created. The poor are here and so are the affluent. We have black and white, international and American, young and old. That is part of what God is doing in this marvelous place."

Since Dr. Wirth's arrival in 1990, the membership of First Church has steadily increased, rising from 2,195 to more than 2,500 by early 1997, and the number of children and youth attending Sunday School has grown from fewer than 100 to an average of 300.

To fund this growth, First Church launched a major capital campaign in 1996. The $6.7 million effort provided for the refurbishment of the sanctuary (revealing the original brick flooring that had been long forgotten and covered), refurbishment of the church facility, and construction of the Christian community center.

In addition to Sunday School, children participate in activities that include choirs, Vacation Bible School, and the Annual Christmas Pageant. The youth participate in Sunday School and other activities that include local service projects, fellowship gatherings, and mission trips to help with building projects and Bible schools. The mission trips have taken them to Mexico, Honduras, Haiti, Jamaica, and a South Dakota Indian reservation. Acknowledging the importance of the young people who will carry First Church into the future, the congregation in 1991 ordained its first youth elder, Elizabeth Dew.

Children at First Church's Haiti mission pause for a moment before resuming their daily activities. Other mission trips have been to Mexico, Honduras, and a South Dakota Indian reservation.

Sanctuary Rededication
May 19, 1996

On a warm spring afternoon, sunlight filtering through the brilliant colors of stained glass windows provides the only illumination in the First Church sanctuary. The muffled whir of traffic on Peachtree Street is the only sound. It is as if the long history of the old church and the cloud of witnesses who have nurtured it exist side-by-side with the hum of the present world that reverberates in the room.

Earlier in the day, in his rededication sermon, Dr. Wirth had quoted the words of Princeton Professor Charles Osgood:

Have you ever wandered into this church . . . when it is empty and silent and you are alone? As you walked quietly about the aisles, or dropped into a pew and sat in solitude, have you ever thought of all that has taken place under this roof? Of the uncounted thousands who, generation after generation, have gathered . . . for prayer and worship?

"The experiences we have shared in this sanctuary," Wirth told the congregation, "the baptisms, confirmations, funerals, memorial services, and wedding celebrations we have attended here, the Sunday services we've enjoyed here, and the hymns and anthems we have sung in this place have overwhelmed us with the sense of God's spirit and the abiding peace and presence of Christ's grace. . . .

"So on this day of rededication of our sanctuary, let us resolve to build upon a firm foundation laid by our forbears and let us recommit our lives to the Lordship of Christ, who is the head and cornerstone of this church. Let us lift up our voices in celebration as we worship God in this holy place, let us renew our determination to serve others in Jesus' name. And above all else, let us never forget that unless the Lord builds the house, those who build it labor in vain.

"In the name of the Father, the Son, and the Holy Spirit. Amen."

Sam Cooper Inman

Dedication of Chapter VI

by Dr. George Wirth and Gayle White

With great gratitude and affection, we dedicate the new chapter of this book to the memory of Sam Cooper Inman, a lifelong member of First Presbyterian Church.

Sam was "dignified and generous and, most importantly, loved and respected by all whose lives he touched," his wife, Florence Ricker Inman, remembers. "He was sensitive and respectful of people from all walks of life."

The son of Hugh T. and Mildred Cooper Inman, Sam was an Atlantan with roots five generations deep in a family that helped shape the city. His grandparents, Edward and Emily MacDougald Inman, built the Swan House, an Atlanta landmark where he lived as a child. In 1913, his great-grandfather, Samuel M. Inman, a founder of Georgia Tech and Agnes Scott College, made possible First Church's purchase of property at Sixteenth and Peachtree Streets.

Sam was a soft-spoken southern gentleman with "impeccable manners" and "a dry sense of humor, which remained with him right up until the end," Florence said. "Although Sam was born with a silver spoon in his mouth, it was important to him to make his own mark, and he did."

After serving in the army during World War II, Sam graduated from the University of Georgia. As a leader in the construction industry, he was president of the Georgia Highway Contractors Association and impressed those who knew him with his integrity, vision, and strong work ethic. He was responsible for building many miles of interstate highway and overseeing other major projects in Georgia and elsewhere.

Continuing a family tradition, he gave generously to Atlanta institutions, including his church. "Sam respected his family's participation in Atlanta's growth and particularly in the growth of First Pres," Florence said.

Sam had two sons, Edward, and John (deceased), six grandchildren, two stepchildren and two stepgrandchildren.

He died at eighty three on August 23, 2010. A gift from his estate underwrote publication of the updated edition of this book.

Chapter VI

The Church in the Heart of the City Reaching Out to the World

Celebrating 150 years of ministry and mission.
— *Founder's Day*
January 11, 1998

Diane and Charlie Whittaker at their retirement reception in August 2010. The Whittakers served as First Church's music directors for twenty-two years.

On January 1, 2000, the world sighed with relief and looked forward with optimism. Predictions of Y2K technological paralysis had failed to materialize, and Americans watched via Atlanta-based CNN as countries around the globe cheered in a new millennium. In his first sermon of the twenty-first century the next day, Dr. George Wirth urged the congregation at First Presbyterian Church of Atlanta to seize the day and the future "with all its promises and possibilities."

The next few years would bring to fruition many promises and possibilities—along with catastrophes, continuing denominational struggles, and a crippling recession. The church would respond to each blessing and challenge as it came, remembering always the theme of the decade: Christ at the Center.

Just two years before, First Church had marked its 150th anniversary with a yearlong schedule of special events. The church, which had once seemed so far from the commercial center of the city, was situated in Midtown, one of metropolitan Atlanta's fastest-developing areas. In the years following the anniversary, a 17th Street Bridge opened across the downtown connector, and Atlantic Station, a massive city-within-a-city, rose up on the site of an abandoned steel mill. But even before a recession stunted growth later in the decade, the very old problems of poverty, homelessness, and hunger lurked beneath the luster of newness. First Church was committed to addressing those needs, and as its members celebrated its sesquicentennial, a new building was taking shape along Sixteenth Street to help meet them. On May 2, 1999, the congregation dedicated the Christian Community Center, made possible by a contribution from member Hal Smith and his family, together with many others, and constructed under the ever-present eye of building committee chairman Jack Stringer, "clerk of the works."

Almost every day, according to Rev. Charles Black, associate pastor for community ministries, men and women in need find help at the community center, also known as the Smith Building. "The three amigos"—members John Marriner, Larry Galindo, and Joseph Wallace—mentor dozens of people each week, assisting them as they apply for Social Security and other benefits. "We're walking beside people until they can pick up and be successful on their own," Marriner said. The Venable Food Pantry and a clothes closet are there, as is the Edna Raine Wardlaw Coker Women's Shelter, nicknamed "The Ritz Carlton" by some residents.

On a floor below the shelter, people find care and support at the Samaritan Counseling Center, established in 1999 with a generous gift from the Rooker family as part of the Colorado-based Samaritan Institute.

Architectural rendering of the Christian Community Center, also known as the Smith Building.

In 2010 the institute presented Dr. Wirth its national award for his role in founding centers in Atlanta and Sewickley, Pennsylvania.

Under the guidance of Dr. Trisha Senterfitt and the Care Ministry Council, the center enhanced the church's ability to care for members, staff, and the wider community.

"Samaritan Counseling Center has been a lifesaver for me and my wife," one patient wrote in a testimonial, "and I mean that literally."

The center's psychologists, psychiatrists, and counselors, who help so many people through losses, faced their own profound grief in 2008 when executive director Dr. Nancy Kirwan died in a car accident. First Church dedicated a lamppost and garden to her memory.

In times of widespread heartbreak and fear, the church can minister just by providing a place for people to gather in their quest for comfort and hope. First Church played that role in the fall of 2001.

On the bright morning of September 11, the staff was trickling into Winship Chapel for regular Tuesday worship. As Dr. Wirth hurried to join them, a television monitor caught his eye. Dumbfounded, he watched the reports: two airliners had flown into the World Trade Center in New York, another into the Pentagon, and yet another had crashed in rural Pennsylvania. Knowing that the world was changing before his eyes, he called the staff to join him. For about an hour they stood transfixed, then quietly joined together for worship where they sang "Our God, Our Help in Ages Past" and prayed.

They knew they must do more. By Friday, a National Day of Prayer, they had planned a service that drew more than twenty-five hundred people from nearby offices and neighborhoods. Those who couldn't squeeze into the sanctuary or crowd into overflow rooms spilled onto the sidewalks outside. Some reached out to touch the old stones of the church as if to pull strength from inside.

That Sunday, Rev. John Claypool delivered the sermon, closing with the promise that "the final sounds of history will not be 'Taps' but 'Reveille.'" But more was to come. The United States was going to war in Afghanistan. Days after bombing began, Dr. Wirth acknowledged that the nation "has been shaken to its core," but reminded the faithful that "the forces of fear are no match against the grace and power and love of God."

Events came full circle nine years later on September 10, 2010, as Atlanta faith leaders met at First Church for a news conference calling for religious tolerance. A Florida pastor had captured attention with a threat to burn the Qur'an in protest of plans for a mosque near Ground Zero in Manhattan. "When one religion is under attack, we're all under attack," said Rev. Gerald Durley, cochairman with Dr. Wirth of the Regional Council of Churches of Atlanta. Dr. Wirth read a statement from Jewish leaders who were celebrating Rosh Hashanah.

The press conference was evidence of First Church's presence in the broader religious community. A bond with The Temple evolved into an am-

Rabbi Alvin Sugarman of The Temple presents Dr. George Wirth with a kiddush cup in commemoration of the church's 150th anniversary. The cup is used weekly in chapel communion services.

O<!-- drop cap -->n a sunny winter Sunday—
Founder's Day 1998—more
than twelve hundred people
poured out of First Presbyterian Church and streamed
down Peachtree Street to the Woodruff
Arts Center for a birthday party marking
the church's 150th anniversary.

"It was an incredible day in
the life of First Presbyterian Church,"
recalled Cindy Candler, cochair of the
event with Leila Taratus.

That was just the beginning.

During the year, the church
would host an evening with Ebenezer
Baptist Church, where Dr. Martin Luther
King Jr. once served. United Methodist
Bishop Bevel Jones and Roman Catholic
Archbishop John Donoghue would
preach from its pulpit. Founding
minister Dr. John Wilson would come
back, bearing a strong resemblance to
actor Tom Key, in an original drama.
And members would reminisce with
former mayor and church member Ivan
Allen Jr. and writers Celestine Sibley

An Anniversary for the Ages

and Rick Allen in a magical night at the Federal Reserve Bank, then on Marietta Street in the spot where the church's first building once stood.

Some anniversary ventures shaped the church for years to come. A breathtaking floral festival and concert sparked enthusiasm for a larger fine arts ministry. Worship with The Temple deepened a desire for interfaith dialogue. And the gift of Grace Chapel to Mount Kenya Academy, a tangible commemoration of the year, sealed life-changing friendships for mission partners in Atlanta and East Africa. First Church has sponsored many trips to Kenya since the chapel dedication.

Another 1998 occasion with significant impact was the ordination and installation of Rev. Craig Goodrich as associate pastor and executive director.

Besides keeping day-to-day operations on track and handling the occasional crisis with the help of his longtime assistant, Pauline Storey, he has revitalized First Church's men's ministry, which by 2011 was touching the lives of more than three hundred men through small groups and fellowship opportunities.

Dr. Wirth and Rev. Goodrich are "a remarkable team," said Doug Ellis, who worked with Rev. Goodrich on a 2005 change in governance that brought the church's trustees into its session.

A lawyer and Washington, D.C., native, Rev. Goodrich moved to Atlanta with his family to attend Columbia Theological Seminary. "I love the people of this church," he said. "I love the staff, and George Wirth has been such a mentor and friend. I love the preaching and teaching. . . . I love looking for God's way through challenges. I actually love going to meetings."

bitious educational project called Reclaiming the Center that pulled the two congregations together under the leadership of the Institute for Christian & Jewish Studies in Baltimore.

The church is also exploring a relationship with nearby Al-Farooq Masjid on Fourteenth Street. "We're very encouraged by the progress made in developing a friendship between the two congregations," Dr. Wirth said.

The partnership between First Church and Hillside Presbyterian Church in Decatur, formed in 2002, was so innovative that it was featured in the denominational magazine *Presbyterians Today*. First Church remains predominantly white, and Hillside is mostly African American, but members of different ethnicities from both congregations work together supporting Hagar's House shelter for women and children, driving relatives to visit prisoners through the Georgia Justice Project, hosting events for participants in DeKalb County's Drug Court, tutoring children through Whiz

Kids, and building Habitat for Humanity houses. "Through the partnership we build bridges, making the kingdom of God more visible here among us," said Rev. Connie Lee, who serves on the staffs of both churches.

The Hillside-First partnership works with Mount Olivet Boys' Home and the Theodora Foundation, a ministry that rescues youths from the sex trade. Both are in Jamaica, one of First Church's five international mission fields. Work began in Haiti in 1990, Kenya in 1995, and Brazil in 1997.

The church's youth and their director, Allison Per-Lee, added Honduras to the list. Annual youth musicals raise money for mission trips in the United States and abroad. The 2011 show was *Hairspray,* and for the first time the cast and crew included youth and leaders from Hillside.

Hundreds of First Church members of all ages have traveled to various mission fields, enriching their own lives, helping partners in other countries, and forming lasting relationships.

Any mission trip can be an adventure,

Volunteers from First Presbyterian Church work on a Habitat for Humanity house. Teams from First Presbyterian helped to build 32 Habitat homes as of 2011.

Hairspray, *the 2011 youth musical, featured a cast from First Church and partner congregation Hillside Presbyterian. The show was the 15th annual musical staged by First Church youth to raise money for mission trips. Elementary-school children at the church have presented nine annual musicals of their own.*

but in January 2010 a contingent to Haiti experienced a disaster that devastated a country. A First Church team was performing health screenings in La Gonâve when they felt the ground shake. About thirty miles away, an earthquake was destroying much of Haiti's capital, Port-au-Prince. Phone lines went dead, and electricity blacked out. In Atlanta, Barb Wirth, a veteran of Haiti missions, served as communications central, collecting information as those in Haiti doled out carefully conserved cell phone power. For two days, until a plane arrived to bring them home, First Church team members held and comforted people in La Gonâve as they heard of dead and missing relatives. "It was terrifying and traumatic for all of us, but not as much as for our sisters and brothers in Haiti," member Sidney West later told the congregation.

Helen Hatch (2nd from left) and Katherine Davey (center) visit with participants of First Church's micro-credit project in Kenya.

Some First Church members do international mission work in their own homes, hosting children with special medical needs through Childspring International, established under that name in 2004. Led by Rose Emily Bermudez, the faith-based nonprofit organization headquartered at the church matches more than 250 children each year with physicians and hospitals in their own countries or in the United States.

The church's commitment to share with people around the world can also be seen in Kenya. After building Grace Chapel at Mount Kenya Academy in 1998 through a faithful gift from Cindy Candler, the church allocated a portion of its 2007 capital campaign to the Presbyterian University of East Africa.

The name of that campaign, "First Things First," expressed the understanding that, in addition to serving others, Christians must be responsible stewards of their resources. For First Church, those resources included a historic building with a leaking roof, dark hallways, outdated equipment, and stones literally falling off its sides.

Doug and Florida Ellis headed the fundraising effort. No target was specified, but "I put a goal of $10 million in mind," Doug Ellis said. To raise members' awareness, the Ellises and their committee conducted tours, pointing out problems. When pledges were tallied, they totaled $15.1 million—enough to do the work, support the Kenya project, and establish an endowment for upkeep. It was the church's second campaign since the community center. In 1999, the church had raised $3 million to buy a parking deck across Peachtree Street. "The Lord blessed us," Ellis said. "All we did was express the need, and a lot of people responded."

John McColl, chairman of the renovation committee, supervised the project, which opened access to some of the church's courtyards (including a memorial garden for cremated remains dedicated in 2003) and created spacious quarters for an expanding music ministry.

Since its founding by Charlie Whittaker as a string ensemble in 1994, the Saint Cecilia Consort has grown into a semiprofessional orchestra. And in 2003 the church added the Presbyterian School for the Performing Arts with classes and private lessons for children and adults. New instruments—four octaves of Whitechapel Handbells in 2006 and a Klop Chamber Organ for Winship Chapel in 2007—enrich the church's worship, as do choirs of all ages.

When Charlie and Diane Whittaker retired in 2010 after twenty-two years as director and associate director of music, respectively, they left the legacy of a thriving program in state-of-the-art facilities.

With its heritage of great music and its location at the center of the arts in Atlanta, First Church is uniquely suited to develop the fine arts as a ministry. The church sponsors events with major arts institutions, hosts tours of private collections, and produces programs such as Musica Sacra concerts and an occasional opera or evening of music.

All ministries of First Church rise out of the will to show love for God and neighbor as Jesus commanded. During the waning of the twentieth century and the beginning of the twenty-first, a program of in-depth Bible study and a theme, "Christ at the Center," undergirded that resolve.

Eve Earnest, then director of Christian education, introduced the church to the multiyear small-group curriculum called Disciple Bible Study in the late 1990s. Some groups became so cemented by collaborative scholarship and personal sharing that they met long after exhausting the Disciple materials. By early 2011 more than six hundred people had been in Disciple groups at First Church.

To sustain the study of the Bible and biblical history at First Church, lifelong member John H. Stembler Jr. left a designated bequest when he died in July 2007. The Stembler Ministry funds opportunities for study, reflection, and renewal such as Disciple Bible Study, "Forum at First" Sunday School classes, Lenten Bible studies, Vacation Bible School, and church retreats with a

biblical theme. It has twice sponsored spiritual immersion experiences with Columbia Seminary.

The theme Christ at the Center grew out of a period of reflection and discernment in the early 2000s. The church was welcoming a more diverse congregation and seeking to meet the needs of a changing community. At the same time, the Presbyterian Church (USA), like many Protestant denominations, was struggling with issues of human sexuality. First Church strived to follow God's will in a time of denominational strife, support its members spiritually, serve the community, and stretch to reach new populations.

In February 2003 the session approved the report of a long-range planning committee headed by Jerry Hassebroek and Roger Neuenschwander. Called *Vision for a Centered Church*, the report emphasized lives centered in Jesus Christ, faith centered in the Reformed tradition, and a church centered in the city.

In her foreword to the document, clerk of session Florida Ellis—the leader who, alongside Dr. Wirth, guided the church through that time—wrote with confidence, "Exciting opportunities lie before us as we live into our vision for

Rev. Craig Goodrich (right) with John Calvin, founder of the Reformed tradition, on the occasion of Calvin's 500th birthday in 2009.

128

the future, always keeping our focus on Christ at the center of our lives and of this church."

First Church's firm tie to its denomination was confirmed when two people related to the church served as moderators of the general assembly in the same decade. Rev. Fahed Abu-Akel, founder of AMIS (the Atlanta Ministry with International Students), who directed the church's mission staff from 1990 to 2001, led the 214th General Assembly in 2002–2003. Rev. Joan Gray was elected by the 217th assembly in 2006 and served as parish associate at First Church during her term.

The twenty-six-hundred-member church remains firmly rooted in its faith while exploring new ways to embrace the future. Its charter members could not have imagined technology that allows people around the world to watch live services on cell phones, hear archived sermons through laptop computers, and even make offerings online.

Dr. Wirth probably didn't imagine that either when he moved to Atlanta in 1990. In 2010 the church marked his twenty years with a dinner and celebration that included a staff skit with a solo by his longtime executive assistant, Martha Olson; tributes from dear friends; and insights into his golf game from three participants in his annual "Pastors' Masters."

Months later, he sat in his office surrounded by hundreds of photographs

Betty Case, cofounder with Anne Neikirk and manager of The Mustard Seed, First Church's book and gift store located in the Smith Building. It is operated entirely by volunteers.

documenting two decades—many taken by him—and reflected on the ministry and mission of First Presbyterian Church. "God has blessed us in so many ways," he said, "and we look forward with great anticipation to the days ahead here at the corner of Sixteenth and Peachtree."

Epilogue

church is more than a building made with bricks and mortar, stained glass, wood and stone. It is a congregation of faithful people who are led by the Holy Spirit. The history of First Presbyterian Church of Atlanta shows that it has been blessed by God in the growing and dynamic community in which it finds itself, and in the gifts and talents conferred upon its members.

Not surprisingly, the history of our church reflects the history of our city. From its beginnings in a log cabin in pre–Civil War Atlanta, the First Presbyterian Church stands now in the midst of a booming metropolis its founding members could not have imagined. During this 150 years, our church has enjoyed periods of peace, progress and prosperity. It has also been challenged by the transition and conflicts of war, race and social division. The church's history shows that, with divine guidance, it has responded by taking a leading role in the development of our community, and in the resolution of its conflicts.

The story of our predecessors, as told in this book, is not just a source of pride, but is also a challenge to us as today's members. The future of the church is held in the hands of God who has promised to guide us and provide for all our needs. We can be sure that God will not fail us. Thanks be to God!

Appendix

This list was compiled from the following church records: an existing 1848–1934 history, session minutes, church rolls, weekly bulletins, minutes from trustees' meetings and internal church correspondence. The completeness of the list for any given pastoral administration is limited by the availability of records from that time. Trustees are listed separately because of the nature of that position and the length of time that many trustees serve.

No attempt has been made to make the lists consistent from era to era (except for spelling out abbreviated names, when the complete names could be verified), nor to bring the list into compliance with current cultural mores (for example, referring to married women by their own names, rather than by their spouse's names exclusively). Names are shown as they appeared in the church records at the time. Where information in the records was inconsistent (not an uncommon occurrence), the best possible attempt was made to reflect the most authoritative record.

1848–1853
Dr. John Simpson Wilson, Stated Supply Pastor
ORGANIZERS OF CHURCH
Keziah Boyd
Margaret Boyd
Henry Brockman
Ruth A. Brockman
C.J. Caldwell
Lucinda Cone
James Davis
Jane Davis
H.A. Fraser
Julia M.L. Fraser
Jane Gill
Annie L. Houston
Oswell Houston
Joel Kelsey
Minerva Kelsey
Harriet Norcross
Joseph Thompson
Mary A. Thompson
Mary J. Thompson
ELDERS
James Davis
Oswell Houston
Joel Kelsey
J.P Logan
O.F. Luckie
William Markham
John Rhea
James Robinson
A.N. Wilson

1853
Rev. John Louis King, Stated Supply Pastor
DEACONS, NO RECORD
ELDERS, NO RECORD

1854
Rev. John E. Dubose, Stated Supply Pastor
DEACONS, NO RECORD
ELDERS, NO RECORD

1855–1858
Rev. John E. Dubose, Pastor
DEACONS, NO RECORD
ELDERS, NO RECORD

1858–1873
Dr. John S. Wilson, Pastor
DEACONS
Leonard Bellingrath
Carl Harmsen
Thomas G. Healey
W.J. Houston
S.B. Hoyt
Samuel M. Inman
Thomas L. Langston
John S. Oliver
J.R. Wallace
ELDERS
Joseph M. Alexander
C.M. Barry
Lucien Bonaparte Davis
Thomas D. Frierson
James Hoge
S.B. Hoyt
Walker P. Inman
Joseph L. King
William M. Lowry
William McMillan
William A. Moore
William Alfred Powell
James Robinson
Berryman D. Shumate
V. Thompson

1874–1882
Dr. Joseph H. Martin, Pastor
DEACONS
Leonard Bellingrath
John B. Daniel
William Hamilton
Carl Harmsen
George W. Harrison
Thomas G. Healey
Samuel M. Inman
Thomas L. Langston
E.F. May
John L. McGaughey
John S. Oliver
ELDERS
Joseph M. Alexander
Lucien Bonaparte Davis
J.G. Earnest
Thomas D. Frierson
James W. Harle
Carl Harmsen
Walker P. Inman
William M. Lowry
George B. McGaughey
William McMillan
William A. Moore
Harvey T. Philips
William Alfred Powell
James Robinson

1882–1883
Rev. Nathan Bachman, Interim Pastor
DEACONS
John B. Daniel
William Hamilton
Carl Harmsen
George W. Harrison
Thomas G. Healey

Thomas L. Langston
E.F. May
John L. McGaughey
ELDERS
Lucien Bonaparte Davis
J.G. Earnest
Thomas D. Frierson
Carl Harmsen
Walker P. Inman
William M. Lowry
George B. McGaughey
William A. Moore
Harvey T. Philips
William Alfred Powell
James Robinson

1883–1898
Dr. Edward Hammett Barnett, Pastor
DEACONS
William Bensel
Wallace W. Boyd
Patrick H. Calhoun
John B. Daniel
William M. Draper
James P. Field
John O. Hamilton
William Hamilton
Carl O. Harmsen Sr.
George W. Harrison
Thomas G. Healey
Augustus M. Hoke
Hugh T. Inman
Thomas L. Langston
E.F. May
John L. McGaughey
J.K. Orr
William A. Speer
John D. Turner
ELDERS
J.W. Bones
Wallace W. Boyd
James M. Collier
John B. Daniel
Lucien Bonaparte Davis
J.G. Earnest
Thomas D. Frierson
Carl Harmsen
Samuel M. Inman
Walker P. Inman
Thomas L. Langston
William M. Lowry
William Markham
George B. McGaughey
William A. Moore
J.S. Panchen
Harvey T. Philips
William A. Powell
James Robinson
John D. Turner

1899–1899
Dr. Richard Orme Flinn, Stated Supply Pastor
DEACONS
William M. Draper
John O. Hamilton
Carl Harmsen
George W. Harrison
J.K. Orr
William A. Speer
ELDERS
J.W. Bones
Wallace W. Boyd
James M. Collier
John B. Daniel
J.G. Earnest
Thomas D. Frierson
Samuel M. Inman
Walker P. Inman
Thomas L. Langston
William Markham
J.S. Panchen
William A. Powell
John D. Turner

1899–1906
Rev. Charles Percy Bridewell, Pastor
DEACONS
S.T. Barnett
C.G. Crewe
Charles L Elyea
Paul L. Fleming
T.B. Gay
C. O. Harmsen
George W. Harrison
William T. Healey
Samuel A. Magill
W.B. Miles
Hugh Richardson
C.R. Winship
John J. Woodside
ELDERS
William Bensel
J.W. Bones
Wallace W. Boyd
C.P. Bridewell
Patrick H. Calhoun
James M. Collier
John B. Daniel
J.G. Earnest
Thomas D. Frierson
Hugh T. Inman
Samuel M. Inman
Walker P. Inman
Thomas L. Langston
Charles H. Lewis
William Markham
J.S. Panchen
W. A. Powell
John D. Turner

1907–1911
Dr. Walter Lee Lingle, Pastor
DEACONS
James R. Bachman
S.W. Carson
R.C. Cassels
Paul L. Fleming
T.B. Gay
G.W. Hampton
William T. Healey
S.J. Magill
W.B. Miles
Gilham H. Morrow
J.A. Shields
Charles W. Wolcott
John J. Woodside
ELDERS
J.R. Bachman
William Bensel
J.W. Bones
Patrick H. Calhoun
S.W. Carson
John B. Daniel
J.G. Earnest
Paul L. Fleming
T.B. Gay
George W. Harrison
William R. Hoyt
Hugh T. Inman
Samuel M. Inman
Walker P. Inman
Thomas L. Langston
Charles H. Lewis
J.E. Nisbet
J.S. Panchen
W.A. Speer
John D. Turner

1912–1914
Rev. Hugh Kelso Walker, Pastor
DEACONS
E.P. Ansley
S.T. Barnett
R.C. Cassels
Charles L. Elyea
D.E. Giffen
G.W. Hampton
Carl O. Harmsen
William T. Healey
P.M. Hubbard
S.J. Magill
William B. Miles
Gilham H. Morrow
William T. Perkerson
Hugh Richardson
J.A. Shields
Chris R. Winship
Charles W. Wolcott
John J. Woodside
ELDERS
James R. Bachman

William Bensel
Patrick H. Calhoun
S.W. Carson
John B. Daniel
John G. Earnest
Paul L. Fleming
T.B. Gay
William R. Hoyt
Samuel M. Inman
Charles H. Lewis
J.E. Nisbet
J.S. Panchen
W.A. Speer

1914–1936
Dr. John Sprole Lyons, Pastor
DEACONS
Jno. C. Allen
E.P. Ansley
H.R. Armstong
S.T. Barnett
Morris Brandon Jr.
H. Grady Brooks
F. Phinizy Calhoun
R.C. Cassels
Charles J. Currie
Dowse B. Donaldson
W.S. Elkin
Charles L. Elyea
Willis T. Everett Jr.
J.P. Fagan
J.A. Fore
S.J. Fuller
D.E. Giffen
G.W. Hampton
Carl O. Harmsen
William T. Healey
Wm. L. Heinz
W.R. Hoyt Jr.
P.M. Hubbard
F.M. Inman
T.H. Latham
T.C. Law
R.G. Lose
S.J. Magill
T.H. McCrea
Dan I. McIntyre
Aubrey Milam
William B. Miles
Max Milligan
Gilham H. Morrow
W.J. Peabody
W.T. Perkerson
E. Owen Perry
Edward D. Powell
Hugh Richardson
J.A. Shields
Charles F. Stone
Homer B. Thompson
Chris R. Winship
Charles W. Wolcott
John J. Woodside Sr.

Paul R. Yopp
H. Lane Young
ELDERS
John C. Allen
James R. Bachman
William Bensel
Edw. S. Burgess
John A. Burgess
Patrick H. Calhoun
S.W. Carson
R.C. Cassels
John B. Daniel
J.G. Earnest
William A. Elliot
Willis M. Everett
Paul L. Fleming
T.B. Gay
Carl O. Harmsen
George W. Harrison
Geo. B. Hoyt
William R. Hoyt Sr.
Samuel M. Inman
Charles H. Lewis
W.L. Little
Curtis C. Lynd
L.J. Magill
J.E. Nisbet
L.M. Norris
J.S. Panchen
Thos. A. Scott
James Sharp
J.W. Smith
William A. Speer
J.J. Timlin
O.C. Wainwright
Edgar Watkins
Philip Weltner
George White
C.R. Winship
George J. Yundt

1936–1952
Dr. William Vardamann Gardner, Pastor
DEACONS
P.D. Allen
Wm.R. Armstong
S.T. Barnett
D.C. Black
P.L. Blackshear
Jos. A. Boatwright
Morris Brandon Jr.
F. Phinizy Calhoun
John M. Cooper
C.C. Cromwell
Charles J. Currie
Hugh F. Dickson
Dowse B. Donaldson
Paul L. Dorn
W.S. Elkin
W.D. Ellis III
C.L. Elyea

Willis M. Everett
J.A. Fore Jr.
James N. Frazer
S.J. Fuller
Edward F. Harrigan
Errol B. Hay Jr.
James R. Henderson
W.R. Hoyt Jr.
Charles D. Hurt
F.M. Inman
Thomas C. Law
Robert G. Lose
Dan I. McIntyre
John F. Magill
T.H. McCrea
Aubrey Milam
Max Milligan
C.E. Mohns
G.H. Morrow
Fritz Orr
E.S. Papy
W.T. Perkerson
E. Owen Perry
Paul M. Potter
J. Edward Powell
Keith A. Quarterman
George B. Raine
Herbert L. Reed
Hal L. Smith
J.W. Stribling
Rock G. Taber
H.B. Thompson
Homer Thompson
J.J. Westbrook
Paul Yopp
H. Lane Young
ELDERS
J.C. Allen
J.R. Bachman
P.L. Blackshear
Edw. S. Burgess
John A. Burgess
Patrick Henry Calhoun
R.C. Cassels
C.F. Clippinger
C.C. Cromwell
Gordon W. Curtiss
Dowse B. Donaldson
Wm. A. Elliot
Wm. D. Ellis
W. Austin Emerson
H.E. Estes
Willis M. Everett
J.K. Fancher
Paul L. Fleming
T.B. Gay Jr.
Erroll B. Hay Jr.
Frank A. Holden
Joseph H. Howey
George B. Hoyt
W.R. Hoyt
Herman Jones Jr.

W.L. Little
J.S. Lyons
W.W. Lyons
L.J. Magill
C.A. Mann
Aubrey Milan
L.M. Norris
E.S. Papy
J.D. Philips
J.L. Rankin
Marthame E. Sanders
T.A. Scott
James Sharp
J.W. Smith
W.A. Speer
Calvin B. Stewart
C.L. Templin
J.J. Timlin
Raymond Turpin
O.C. Wainwright
Edgar Watkins
Robt. C. Watkins
Philip Weltner
Edw. S. White
George White
K.D. White
L.E. Williams
Paul R. Yopp
George J. Yundt

1952–1953
Interim Pastor Not Appointed
DEACONS
Wm. R. Armstrong
D.C. Black
Jos. H. Boatwright
Morris Brandon Jr.
F. Phinizy Calhoun
John M. Cooper
Charles J. Currie
Hugh F. Dickson
Paul L. Dorn
C.L. Elyea
Willis M. Everett
J.A. Fore Jr.
James H. Frazer
S.J. Fuller
James R. Henderson
Charles D. Hurt
Thomas C. Law
Robert G. Lose
Dan I. McIntyre
John F. Magill
C.E. Mohns
G.H. Morrow
Fritz Orr
E. Owen Perry
J. Edward Powell
Keith A. Quarterman
George B. Raine
Herbert L. Reed
Hal L. Smith

J.W. Stribling
H.B. Thompson
Homer Thompson
J.J. Westbrook
H. Lane Young
ELDERS
J.C. Allen
J.R. Bachman
P.L. Blackshear
C.F. Clippinger
C.C. Cromwell
Gordon W. Curtiss
Dowse B. Donaldson
Wm. A. Elliott
Wm. D. Ellis
W. Austin Emerson
H.C. Estes
J.K. Fancher
Paul L. Fleming
T.B. Gay Jr.
Erroll B. Hay Jr.
Frank A. Holden
Joseph H. Howey
George B. Hoyt
Herman Jones Jr.
L.J. Magill
C.A. Mann
Aubrey Milam
E.S. Papy
William L. Pressly
Marthame E. Sanders
Calvin B. Stewart
Raymond Turpin
O.C. Wainwright
Robt. C. Watkins
Edw. S. White
K.D. White
L.E. Williams
Paul R. Yopp

1953–1976
Dr. Harry Amos Fifield, Pastor
DEACONS
John C. Ager
C. Scott Akers
Frank W. Allcorn III
Ivan Allen Jr.
Wm. R. Armstrong
Wm. F. Arthison
C. Thomas Bagley
Clifford D. Bailey
William M. Barber
D.C. Black
Bates Block
Joseph H. Boatwright
Mrs. Thomas V. Bockman
Thomas B. Branch III.
Morris Brandon Jr.
Owen V. Braun
Russell J. Brooke
Austin Brown
James Pope Brown

W. Wheeler Bryan
Mrs. A. Paul Cadenhead
F. Phinizy Calhoun
Lawson P. Calhoun
Mrs. W. Cothan Campbell
Robert L. Carmichael
Frank Carter Jr.
Louis L. Cason
James Reid Conyers
John M. Cooper
Joseph W. Cooper Jr.
Samuel I. Cooper
Dallas M. Covington
Michael C. Crawford
Charles E. Cunningham
Charles J. Currie
Charles J. Currie Jr.
Gordon W. Curtiss Jr.
John C. Dabney
Frank T. Davis
Dale Dewberry
Hugh F. Dickson
Mrs. Tom Dillon
R.B. Dorman Jr.
Paul L. Dorn
Hugh M. Dorsey Jr.
Hamilton Douglas Jr.
David L. Drake
Jesse Draper
Mrs. Charles S. Dudley
Robert S. Duggan
Thomas K. Edenfield
Charles L. Elyea
George D. Elyea
Mrs. George D. Elyea
Robert E. Eskew
Mrs. Robert E. Eskew
Willis M. Everett
John T. Ferguson
R.B. Fogarty
Theodore M. Forbes Jr.
J. Albert Fore Jr.
James N. Frazer
Samuel G. Friedman Jr.
S.J. Fuller
Cline D. Futch
Cline D. Futch Jr.
David H. Gambrell
Robert L. Garges
William M. Gibson
James Gough Jr.
Edward P. Gould
Henry W. Grady
Henry W. Grady Jr.
Robert S. Grady
Albert Griffin Jr.
Wm.E. Hamilton
William A. Hanger
Allen S. Hardin
Mary Bradley Hay
James R. Henderson
Charles L. Henry

Ralph H. Hester
Thomas D. Hills
G. Arthur Howell Jr.
Charles C. Hull
J. Gibson Hull
Charles D. Hurt
Frank M. Inman Jr.
McChesney Hill Jeffries
Francis G. Jones Jr.
Herman Jones Jr.
Blaine Kelley Jr.
Talley Kirkland
John C. Knupp
Charles Raymond Kyle
Robert J. Kyle
Thomas C. Law
Ernest L. Lewis
Alfred H. Lloyd
James W. Lockwood
Robert G. Lose
Dan I. McIntyre
John F. Magill
Frank H. Maier Jr.
H.G. Mann
J. Wesley Martin
Robert Carr Martin
George W. Mathews Jr.
Harold S. McConnell
Mrs. Harold S. McConnell
Sam D. McDaniel Jr.
Phil C. McDuffie Jr.
Paul W. McGaughy
James A. McKibben Jr.
Hugh B. McPhail
C. Edwin Medlock
C.E. Mohns
A. Currie Monroe
George Richard Moore
Alec C. Morgan
Gilham H. Morrow
Edward Allen Moulthrop
William W. Neal
John T. Nesbitt
Ben L. O'Callaghan
Fritz Orr
A.B. Padgett
A.N. Park
Arthur A. Paty III
Mark P. Pentecost
E. Owen Perry
Henry Wellborn Persons
Robert C. Petty
J. Edward Powell
Keith A. Quarterman
George B. Raine
Herbert L. Reed
William B. Reeves
Hugh I. Richardson Jr.
Barney L. Rickenbacker
Robert E. Robinson
William A. Rooker
Mrs. Wm. Jack Sadler

William W. St. Clair
Marhame Sanders Jr.
James Sartor
Edward L. Savell
Mrs. Edward L. (Bettie) Savell
Thomas J. Schermerhorn
F.W. Schultz Jr.
William B. Shartzer
L. Miles Sheffer
W.E. Shelburne
Hal L. Smith
John D. Smith
J.W. Stribling
John W. Talley Jr.
Kenneth S. Taratus
Harry B. Thompson Jr.
Harry B. Thompson III
Homer Thompson
J. Alston Thompson
Rutledge Tufts
J. Frank Walker
Frank Ogden Walsh Jr.
William C. Wardlaw Jr.
Robert G. Watt
Herbert J. West
J.J. Westbrook
James J. White
James R. Wilkinson
Alva S. Wilson
John C. Wilson
James G. Wohlford
J. P. Woodall
William S. Woods
Charles C. Workman Jr.
Dom H. Wyant
Edwin F. Yancey Jr.
H. Lane Young
William D. Young
George J. Yundt Jr.

ELDERS
Fred L. Ackerson
Harry Y. Alexander
John C. Allen
Herbert S. Archer III
William R. Armstrong
J.R. Bachman
William H. Barber
Jarvis Barnes
Perry L. Blackshear
E. Richard Bollinger Jr.
Thomas B. Branch III
Russell J. Brooke
James Pope Brown
Robert L. Brown
Mrs. Robert L. Brown
A. Paul Cadenhead
F. Phinizy Calhoun Jr.
Lawson P. Calhoun
Louie L. Cason
Frederick O. Church
Thomas Hal Clarke
Charles F. Clippinger

Robert C. Commander
C.T. Conyers
Vernon D. Crawford
C.C. Cromwell
Mrs. Charles E. (Nancy) Cunningham
Charles J. Currie Jr.
Gordon W. Curtiss
Frank T. Davis
Jefferson Davis
Dowse B. Donaldson
Hugh M. Dorsey Jr.
David B. Drake
Talmage L. Dryman
Robert S. Duggan Jr.
George T. Duncan
William M. Earnest
Lawrence L. Edge
Lawrence L. Edge Jr.
William A. Elliott
William D. Ellis Sr.
Wm. Douglas Ellis Jr.
Mrs. William D. Ellis Jr.
W. Austin Emerson
Hansell P. Enloe
Robert E. Eskew
Harald C. Estes
James K. Fancher
Paul L. Fleming
John E. Fontaine
J. Albert Fore Jr.
John O. Gaultney
David H. Gambrell
Frank B. Garner
T. Bolling Gay
Charles Gowen
C. Bruce Gregory
Mrs. Albert Griffin Jr.
William A. Hanger
Lennart L. Hanson
W. Richard Hauenstein
Erroll B. Hay Jr.
James Ross Henderson
Fred A. Henninger
Mrs. Robert L. Hinds
Frank A. Holden
William I. Holland
W. I. Howell
Joseph H. Howey
George B. Hoyt
Samuel E. Hudgins
J. Gibson Hull
Charles D. Hurt
Mrs. Charles D. Hurt Sr.
McChesney H. Jeffries
William H. Jentzen
Herman Jones Jr.
Blaine Kelley Jr.
Talley Kirkland
John C. Knupp
Robert J. Kyle
Rayford P. Kytle Jr.
Donald A. Leslie

Richard H. Lyle
Clarence A. Mann
Hobart G. Mann
Willing B. Manning Jr.
J. Wesley Martin
Devereaux F. McClatchey Jr.
Mrs. Sam D. (Betsy) McDaniel Jr.
John W. Merry
Aubrey Milam
Mrs. George A. Moore
William W. Neal
Fritz Orr
A.B. Padgett
Elfred S. Papy
O.J. Parker Jr.
Arthur A. Paty Jr.
Samuel W. Perry
J. Wm. Pinkston
William L. Pressly
Richard H. Pretz
George B. Raine
Baxter S. Rains Jr.
Thomas N. Rains
Ed Reeves
Barney L. Rickenbacker
Marthame E. Sanders
Edward L. Savell
John C. Settlemayer
L. Miles Sheffer
Hal L. Smith
Russell A. Smith
Calvin B. Stewart
Allan E. Strand
D. Glenn Sudderth
Donald G. Thomas
Charles L. Towers
Rutledge Tufts
Raymond Turpin
Paul K. Vonk
Bill C. Wainwright
C.C. Wainwright
J. Frank Walker
Frank O. Walsh Jr.
Henderson C. Ward
William C. Wardlaw
Robert C. Watkins Jr.
Robert C. Watt
Robert G. Watt Sr.
R. Baker Weidinger
Herbert J. West
Joseph J. Westbrook
Edward S. White
K.D. White
James H. Whitten
L.E. Williams
James G. Wohlford
Mrs. James G. (Mary) Wohlford
Dom H. Wyant
Paul R. Yopp
James Blake Young Jr.

1976–1977
Interim Pastor Not Appointed
Moderator, William L. Pressly
DEACONS
C. Scott Akers
Herber S. Archer III
Mrs. Thomas V. Bockman
W. Wheeler Bryan
Mrs. A. Paul (Sara) Cadenhead
Mrs. W. Cothan (Anne) Campbell
James Reid Conyers
Dallas M. Covington
Michael C. Crawford
Charles E. Cunningham
Susan Daugherty
Mrs. Tom Dillon
R.B. Dorman Jr.
Mrs. George D. Elyea
Mrs. Robert E. (Iris) Eskew
John T. Ferguson
Cline D. Futch Jr.
William M. Gibson
James Gough Jr.
Edward P. Gould
C. Bruce Gregory
Mary Bradley Hay
Ralph H. Hester
Thomas D. Hills
Mrs. Robert L. (Isabella) Hinds
Charles Raymond Kyle
Donald A. Leslie
Ernest L. Lewis
James W. Lockwood
L. Gillis MacKinnon III
Frank H. Maier Jr.
George W. Mathews Jr.
Mrs. Harold S. (Marianna) McConnell
G. Richard Moore
Ben L. O'Callaghan
A.B. Padgett
A.N. Park
Robert C. Petty
Daniel S. Rees
William B. Reeves
Mrs. William Jack (Susie) Sadler
Mrs. Edward L. (Bettie) Savell
Thomas J. Schermerhorn
A.B. Simms III
A. Jack Stringer
John W. Talley Jr.
Kenneth S. Taratus
Harry B. Thompson III
John A. Woodall
William David Young

ELDERS
Herbert S. Archer III
William H. Barber Sr.
E. Richard Bollinger Jr.
Thomas B. Branch III
Russell J. Brooke
James Pope Brown
Mrs. Robert L. (Alice) Brown

Mrs. Charles E. (Nancy) Cunningham
Charles J. Currie Jr.
Jefferson Davis
Hugh M. Dorsey Jr.
David B. Drake
Talmage Lamar Dryman
Robert S. Duggan Jr.
William M. Earnest
Lawrence L. Edge Jr.
Mrs. Wm. Douglas (Florida) Ellis
Hansell P. Enloe
David H. Gambrell
Frank B. Garner
Mrs. Albert Griffin Jr.
Mrs. Charles D. (Melissa) Hurt Sr.
McChesney H. Jeffries
Blaine Kelley Jr.
John C. Knupp
Hobart G. Mann
William B. Manning Jr.
Mrs. Samuel D. (Betsy) McDaniel Jr.
Mrs. George A. (Isabelle) Moore
William L. Pressly
Barney L. Rickenbacker
William W. St. Clair
L. Miles Sheffer
Mrs. Thomas D. (Eunice) Sims
Allan E. Strand
Mrs. Rutledge (Mimi) Tufts
Mrs. Raymond (Winifred) Turpin
Bill C. Wainwright
J. Frank Walker
Frank O. Walsh Jr.
Henderson C. Ward
William C. Wardlaw
Robert C. Watkins Jr.
Robert G. Watt Sr.
Edward S. White
Mrs. James G. (Mary) Wohlford
Dom H. Wyant
James Blake Young Jr.

1977–1988
Dr. Paul Thornton Eckel, Pastor
DEACONS
C. Scott Akers
Nack Young An
Herbert S. Archer III
Wheeler Bryan
Sara D. Cadenhead
Mrs. W. Cothan (Anne) Campbell
James Reid Conyers
Dallas M. Covington
Michael C. Crawford
Charles C. Cunningham
James E. Cushman
Susan Daugherty
Mary Joe Dellinger
R.B. Dorman
Iris Eskew
William M. Gibson
James Gough

Henry W. Grady Jr.
C. Bruce Gregory
Mary Bradley Hay
James R. Henderson
Ralph H. Hester
Thomas D. Hills
Mrs. Robert L. (Isabella) Hinds
Charles Raymond Kyle
Donald A. Leslie
C. Linden Longino Jr.
L. Gillis MacKinnon III
Frank H. Maier Jr.
George W. Mathews Jr.
Marianna McConnell
Norman F. Miller
G. Richard Moore
Ben L. O'Callaghan
A.B. Padgett
Robert C. Petty
Daniel S. Rees
William B. Reeves
Mrs. William Jack (Susie) Sadler
Bettie Savell
Thomas J. Schermerhorn
A.B. Simms Jr
A. Jack Stringer
Kenneth S. Taratus
Harry B. Thompson III
J. Aston Thompson
Lenox (Tom) Thornton
John A. Woodall
William D. Young

ELDERS
C. Scott Akers
Helen Akers
Nack Young An
D. Reed Andrew
Emily Archer
Herbert S. Archer III
Albert Y. Badre
Clifford Bailey
Elizabeth M. Balthis
Martha J. Banks
William H. Barber Sr.
Jarvis Barnes
Charles Bedford
Nancy Bedford
James L. Bentley
Frances S. Bockman
E. Richard Bollinger Jr.
Carl A. Bramlette
Thomas B. Branch III
Russell J. Brooke
James Pope Brown
Robert L. Brown
Mrs. Robert L. (Alice) Brown
Elizabeth G. (Libby) Browne
Robert A. Browne
Jean Davis Bynum
A. Paul Cadenhead
Sara D. Cadenhead
F. Phinizy Calhoun Jr.

Lawson P. Calhoun
Robert W. Candler Jr.
Julian S. Carr Jr.
Victor A. Cavanaugh
J. Caleb Clarke III
Mary Clarke
Ike W. Cobb
J. Reid Conyers
Dallas M. Covington
Pam A. Covington
Michael C. Crawford
Charles E. Cunningham
Nancy A. Cunningham
Charles J. Currie Jr.
Russell H. Dabney
Susan Daugherty
Jefferson Davis
Mary Joe Dellinger
Brown W. Dennis
E. Dale Dewberry
Virginia G. Dewberry
Mary Doom
David B. Drake
Talmage L. Dryman
Kathleen R. Duggan
Robert S. Duggan Jr.
George T. Duncan
LaTrelle R. Duncan
Eve Anderson Earnest
William M. Earnest
Lawrence L. Edge Jr.
Lee Edwards
Donald J. Ellis
Florida S. Ellis.
William Douglas Ellis Jr.
Hansell P. Enloe
Iris H. Eskew
Robert E. Eskew
Margaret V. Fancher
Virginia P. Ferguson
Michael Franchot
Betty Franklin
David H. Gambrell
Luck Gambrell
Frank B. Garner
Righton B. Gordy
Nancy D. Gould
Charles L. Gowen
Henry W. Grady Jr.
Charles P. Graham
C. Bruce Gregory
Albert Griffin Jr.
Mrs. Albert Griffin Jr.
George A. Grove
Earl Haltiwanger Jr.
William A. Hanger
Lennart L. Hanson
W. Richard Hauenstein
Linda L. Hawk
Edith Henderson
James R. Henderson
Thomas D. Hills

Norris L. Hogans Sr.
Ellis C. Hooper
Arthur Howell
Samuel E. Hudgins
Melissa J. Hurt
McChesney H. Jeffries
David G. Jones
Blaine Kelley Jr.
Sylvia S. Kelley
John C. Knupp
Robert J. Kyle
George Lancaster
Jean W. Lemonds
Donald A. Leslie Jr.
P. Harvey Lewis
J. Charles Lockwood
C. Linden Longino
L. Gillis MacKinnon
Patricia S. Mallory
Hobart G. Mann
Jane J. Manning
William B. Manning Jr.
Devereaux F. McClatchey
Harold S. McConnell
Marianna D. McConnell
Betsy D. McDaniel
Michael J. McDevitt
Susan M. Mendheim
Harmon B. Miller III
Norman F. Miller
Mrs. George A. (Isabelle) Moore
Ben O'Callaghan
A.B. Padgett
Mark P. Pentecost Jr.
Jerry G. Peterson
Robert C. Petty
William L. Pressly
C. Tom Reeder
Daniel S. Rees
William B. Reeves
William E. Rice
Barney L. Rickenbacker
Dudley C. Rochelle
Jean Russ
William W. St. Clair
Bettie H. Savell
Edward L. Savell
Bron Gayna Schmit
L. Miles Sheffer
Gary B. Shell
Edward H. Shirley
A.B. Simms III
Eunice H. Sims
Hal L. Smith
John D. Smith
P. Andrew Springer
Martha Ann Stegar
Allan E. Strand
A. Jackson (Jack) Stringer
John E. Talmadge
J. Alston Thompson
Charles E. Towers

Mrs. Rutledge (Mimi) Tufts
Winifred Turpin
Bill C. Wainwright
Frank O. Walsh Jr.
Henderson C. Ward
Robert C. Watkins Jr.
Robert G. Watt
Joe Westbrook
Edward S. White
Richard N. Whittier
John F. Williams
Kit Williams
Tom Withycombe
James G. Wohlford
Mary G. Wohlford
John D. Wolfe
John A. Woodall
Dom H. Wyant
David E. York
J. Blake Young Jr.
William D. Young

1988–1990
Dr. James Davison Philips, Interim Pastor
ELDERS
Emily Archer
C. William Austin III
Albert Y. Badre
Nancy Bedford
James L. Bentley
Carl A. Bramlette
Elizabeth G. (Libby) Browne
A. Paul Cadenhead
Robert W. Candler Jr.
Mary Clarke
Ike W. Cobb
Pam A. Covington
Charles E. Cunningham
Mary Joe Dellinger
Brown W. Dennis
E. Dale Dewberry
Anne Drake
LaTrelle Duncan
William M. Earnest
George P. Edwards
W. Douglas Ellis
Iris Eskew
Richard R. Felker
John T. Ferguson
Michael Franchot
Betty Franklin
Charles P. Graham
A. George Grove III
David F. Hale
W. Richard Hauenstein
George J. Hauptfuhrer III
William G. Hays Jr.
Ellis C. Hooper
J. Robert Howard
Martha Hunter
Jethro H. Irby III

David G. Jones
George W. Lancaster
Donald A. Leslie Jr.
P. Harvey Lewis
Floyd O. Lohr
Jack T. Mallory Jr.
Susan M. Mendheim
Roger Neuenschwander
Jerry G. Peterson
Dudley C. Rochelle
Leslie J. Rodriguez
Jean Russ
Gary B. Shell
Edward H. Shirley
John D. Smith
A. Jackson (Jack) Stinger
John E. Talmadge
Richard N. Whittier
John F. Williams
Tom Withycombe
Dom H. Wyant
Connie York
C.W. (Buddy) Young Jr.

1990–present
Dr. George Bryant Wirth, Pastor
ELDERS
Fouad G. Abu-Akel
Helen Akers
Sue Anthony
Robert Antonisse
Emily Archer
Mary Skinner Archer
Jean Austin
C. William Austin III
Rene Austin
Jarvis Barnes
Claire Barry
Wesley Barry
Kathy Beard
Eleanor W. Beckman
Charles Bedford
Nancy Bedford
Stephanie Benson
James Bentley
N. Edward Birchfield Jr.
Christopher D. Black
David C. Black III
Lisa Bondurant
Peter Boorn Jr.
Alex Booth
Jeff Bramlett
Carl A. Bramlette
Tom Branch
Frank Brannon
James R. Bryant Jr.
Clancy Buckler
Jim Buckler
Susan Buell
Susan Bulit
Darsey Butler
G. Bland Byrne

A. Paul Cadenhead
Meg Campbell
Nancy H. Campbell
Cindy Candler
Karna Candler
Robert W. Candler Jr.
Sally Cannon
George E. Case III
George (Ned) Case II
Barbara Cavanaugh
Vic Cavanaugh
Jim Claffey
Katherine Clarke
Mary Clarke
Ike W. Cobb
Allison Cochran
Jim Coil
Liz Cook
C. Peter Cooley
Jeffery Couch
Greg Council
Ann Cox
Nancy Culp
Charles Cunningham
Nancy Cunningham
Susan Daugherty
Katherine Davey
Sara H. Deiters
Mary Joe Dellinger
Brown Dennis
Carol Dew
Elizabeth Dew
James Dew
E. Dale Dewberry
Anne Drake
LaTrelle Duncan
Ann DuPre
Norman DuPre
Walter E. DuPre III
Bill Earnest
Merrill Earnest
William Earnest
Beth Edwards
Elizabeth Edwards
George Edwards
Lee Edwards
Emery Ellinger III
Doug Ellis
Florida Ellis
Iris Eskew
Margaret Evans
Anne Farrisee
Richard Felker
John T. Ferguson
Carla Ferrell
Debby Finkle
Rayburn Fisher Jr.
Lloyd Flood
Nancy Frampton
Mike Franchot
John Freebairn
Kathleen Freebairn

Townshend Fugitt
Larry Galindo
Charles Ginden
Nancy D. Gould
Harry Grady III
Tom Greene
Al Griffin
A. George Grove III
David F. Hale
Jim Hasson
W. Richard Hauenstein
George J. Hauptfuhrer III
Connie Hawkins
William G. Hays Jr.
Quill Healy II
Carlton Henson
Thomas D. Hills
Norris Hogans
Yvonne Hogans
Ellis Hooper
Charlie Houk
Don Houk
Dot Houk
Susan Hovis
J. Robert Howard
John Howard
Jordan Howard
Clark Howell
Florida Huff
Martha Hunter
David W. Inglis
Jethro H. Irby III
Laurie Irby
Ginger Jeffies
Vesta Jones
Forde Kay
Robert Kerr
Sal Kibler
Nancy Kirwan
Gail Kitchens
Stevie Knox
Martha Kollme
George W. Lancaster
Duggan Lansing
John Lansing
Jeffrey Y. Lewis
P. Harvey Lewis
Tad Little

Floyd O. Lohr
Patricia E. (Pat) Lummus
Jack T. Mallory Jr.
John Marriner
Judy Martin
Guerry Mashburn
John McColl
Harold S. McConnell
Steve McMillan
Cindy Meade
Sandy Miller
Lawrence Mock
Joel Moore
Jim Morgens
Ginny Munger
Tom Munger
Margaret Murphy
Martha Neal
Anne Neikirk
John Neuenschwander
Leann Neuenschwander
Roger Neuenschwander
Karen Nevin
Eddie Newsom
Julia Newsom
Guerry Norwood
Karen Papy
Scott Patterson
O. Bradley Payne
Mark Pentecost
Dorothy Peterson
Jerry Peterson
Nancy Peterson
Betty Piephoff
Elizabeth Piephoff
Brenda Crayton-Pitches
Stephen Pitches
Jenny Pomeroy
David Pope
Madison Pratt
Allison Prickett
James E. Prickett
Jenny Rankin
M. Timothy Renjilian
Susan Richards
Leslie J. Rodriguez
Mike Russ
Nell Ryan

Betty Morgan Sanders
Jesse Sasser Jr.
Claire Schwahn
John Seeds
Adele Shepherd
Charlotte Shields
Tom Shields
Ted Shirley
Harry Sibley
Jack N. Sibley
John D. Smith
John E. Smith
Margy Smith
Richard A. Smith
Rush S. Smith
Brian Soderberg
Donald C. (Don) Spencer Jr
Melissa Spender
Beth Stanford
Jack Stinger
Frank Strickland
Donna Tabaka
John W. (Jack) Talley Jr
John Talmadge
Margaret Talmadge
Kenneth Taratus
Tom Tye
Joseph Wallace
Henderson C. Ward
David Watson
John Webster
Julie H. Webster
Woodrow Wells
Ansley Whipple
Gayle White
Richard N. Whittier
Hollis Wise
Kathy Withycombe
Tom Withycombe
Ginny Wohlford
Ellen Adair Wyche
Connie York
David York
Blake Young
Carol Young
C.W. (Buddy) Young Jr.
Zack Young
Kendall J. (Ken) Zeliff Jr.

Index